BLINDWALK
TO POTTER'S FARM
An Odyssey of Spirit

DIANE BRANDER

First published May, 1996 by Windspirit Press in cooperation with Brander and Associates. P.O. Box 864, Washburn, Wisconsin 54891, 715.373.2988.

Fourth Printing, May 1998

Printed in the United States of America
ISBN 0-9640177-8-4

Windspirit Press, P.O. Box 6, Washburn, Wisconsin
Cover Photos by Craig Blacklock, Moose Lake, Minnesota
Cover Design by David Garon, Digital Ink, Duluth, Minnesota
Layout and Printing by Joel Hoefle, Digital Marketing, Minneapolis, Minnesota

THIS BOOK IS DEDICATED TO
MY ASSOCIATES
AND TO MAVIS SUTTON,
WHO TAUGHT ME SO MUCH WHILE SHE
WAS ON EARTH.
HER CONTINUED PRESENCE
IN SPIRIT IS MUCH APPRECIATED.

EARTHLY ACKNOWLEDGMENTS

There are numerous folks who deserve a resounding thank you. First, to my editor John Kalbrener who had every reason to throw in the towel after reading the first draft of this manuscript. Instead he has honored me with perseverance, wit, energy, wisdom and love. I would not have completed this project without his support.

Thanks to those who agreed to review the roughed-out versions and offer commentary and feedback. Included are Brenda, Kay, Marilyn, Melanie, Rebecca, Sandi, Terry, Bob, Scott, Ann, Dan and Tara. And to Fred Ingles who thought this idea was the right idea. Thanks also to Skip and Jill who, along with many others, have offered their encouragement and their love through the Board of Trust and volunteers of Potter's Farm.

Namaste to Amani who read the final version and put her wholehearted support as well as her publishing company, Windspirit Press, behind the project.

I thank Brenda who allowed the summary of her Earth Life Wheel to be included in the final chapter, and Annie, whose transformation is partially chronicled near the close of the book.

Thanks also to my spiritual partners, Anawan and Buffalo Man. And deep gratitude for the appearance of Joel, who has offered various forms of support in the printing of the book, all in the name of Karma, says he.

Finally, I acknowledge my earth-family: my partner Bob, who traveled the length, breadth and depth of this odyssey with patience, stamina, courage and love; and to our children, Catherine, Tara and Scott as well as my unforgettable mother-in-law Jean. It is truly remarkable that we can all be teachers and students together.

I AM within you. I AM not more in one soul than in another; it is simply a matter of awareness. Some souls are more aware of the divinity within them than others and are able to draw from that source and live by that source. Therefore they appear to be living and demonstrating something supernatural. There is nothing supernatural about it; it is simply living by My laws, using the power that is within each one as it should be used. Air is there to be breathed, but it is up to you to breathe it in. Electricity is there to be used, but it has to be harnessed and then switched on and used. Otherwise the electricity is there but it does not demonstrate its power which is waiting to be released. So with the spiritual power within you. It is there for you to use, but unless you plug in and switch on that power, there it remains.

Eileen Caddy
Opening Doors Within

CONTENTS

PROLOGUE

This book is a personal journey. I share miracles, and pilgrimage and practical voices of Spirit. It is offered to those of you on a similar spiritual quest in the hope that you will declare your own stories worth sharing. Perhaps you will also find that they are not as strange as you might have thought.

Before we begin, you must realize that I, like you, am an imperfect person. I have fear attacks and am needy beyond belief sometimes. I'm just not as fearful or needy as I used to be. That feels good.

I try to live life to the hilt every moment of every day and sometimes that strength of commitment and zeal can get me into all sorts of trouble. As others are fond of saying, I can come on very strong. But I am now aware that it is also that strength and that sense of adventure that has allowed all of the events I am going to share with you to unfold, and that I wouldn't change for the world.

This journey I'm going to try to share with you as honestly and openly as I can is a love story. But not the mushy kind. It's about a relationship that began as "just another special relationship," snarled by strife, lust, and power issues and many ups and many downs. But this love story takes a turn and the purpose becomes holy. And then things really get out of whack, because we are <u>not</u> used to that purpose! So it's pretty much been an uphill struggle ever since. But I think for the first time in my life, I'm finally beginning to understand what love is all about. That surely makes it worthwhile.

I do not use traditional terms in traditional ways. I'm a Christian by upbringing and I continue to experience Jesus as my Brother and Way shower. But it appears that a lot has been convoluted through the years. I believe that humankind has imposed its own views on what was revealed 2000 years ago as a natural, powerful yet revolutionary way to live in this world. The cross, to me, is a symbol of liberation. Its shape is a daily reminder of the need for balance between heaven and earth. With balance, grounding and centering we can walk in harmony with all of Creation.

I believe that errors are for correcting, not getting bent out of shape over. And guilt is for those who think that we are created imperfect and will never make the grade.

The same goes for judgement. I certainly have enough responsibility taking care of me without worrying about others and what choices they make in their lives. I can feel empathy and I can care deeply but I can't change others or the way they feel or the path they choose. I don't have the first clue to what's in their overall best interest or what lessons they may need to learn.

Therefore I appreciate it when others do not judge me and ask things of me that I cannot give, either because I'm just not there yet or I'm no longer choosing that for myself. I can only have one Ultimate Inspiration and that is God. And God gives me complete freedom of will. The secret seems to be though, that when God and I are in synchrony of wills, things truly hum.

When I refer to God, I also call God by "All That There Is," "Great Spirit" and assorted other terms that help me cope with The Enormity Of It All. I believe Holy Spirit is a unified collection of practical voices for God that truly assist us daily in our journey. And I believe Angels and other spirits exist in my world. I trust they do in yours as well.

While writing *Blindwalk* I've had to wrestle with the notion that sharing my personal story could be seen as an egotistical ploy. During a period of great doubt, I was gifted with Brenda Ueland's book, *If You Want to Write,* and was thrilled to hear her spirit speak to us about this very issue. So please, as she wisely advises, remember that if you should decide this isn't worth reading, simply put down the book and walk away. But if you find it worthwhile? Well then, darlin', we're in business.

In Brenda Ueland's words:

... at last I understood from William Blake and VanGogh and other great men, and from myself — from the truth that is in me (and which I have at last learned to declare and stand up for, as I am trying to persuade you to stand up for your inner truth) — at last I understood that writing was this: an impulse to share with other people a feeling or truth that I myself had. Not to preach to them, but to give it to them if they cared to hear it. If they did not - fine. They did not need to listen. That was alright too... When I learned all this then I could write freely and jovially and not feel contracted and guilty about being such a conceited ass...

ORIGIN OF BLINDWALKING

To trust in the force that moves the universe is faith. Faith isn't blind. It's visionary. Faith is belief that the universe is on our side, and that the universe knows what it's doing.
Marianne Williamson

[Faith] is not a visionless, unaware obedience to outside forces and pressures. It's Faith. "Blind faith" some say. In fact, there is no other kind at this high level; if it weren't blind it wouldn't be faith.
Jack Hawley

The paradox of the universe is that both of the above are true.
D.B.

Blindwalking is a term frequently used to describe an outdoor exercise of faith done in partnership. During the '60s and '70s I took part in blindwalks several times. The whole idea is to experience being in a state of dependency in an unfamiliar situation. You must learn to trust your partner who is asked to lead you on an extensive outdoor walk while you are blindfolded. If your partner is gentle and caring as well as imaginative, the experience is exhilarating. I always thought it was a given that the partner in the exercise would be trustworthy, so I joined without hesitation. Then in the early 70's I witnessed an example of cruelty.

This time a young woman's male partner deliberately walked her into trees, and up and down stairways without warning. The woman finally became unnerved enough to remove her blindfold, refusing to go any further. She was crying and his angry ego was showing.

After this fearful encounter I stopped participating or using this exercise for several years. It was in 1988 that I was again asked to join in a blindwalk with a group of folks engaged in leadership training in Colorado. The exercise was profoundly moving for me. Not only was it a loving experience, but I realized that I had been on just such a walk of faith with God for the past four years of my life. The parallels with the failed walk are there as well. Many times I have felt fearful that the amount of trust we must place in the complete walk with God is just too dangerous or appears futile; mostly because I have chosen to follow the wrong leads. I now know there is a better way.

INTRODUCTION

When did it start? Was it the instant of my birth or was experiencing rebirth essential? Perhaps it germinated in the safety of the old Presbyterian church in Stillwater, Minnesota when I was a child. But even then it seemed vague and distant except in rare moments when a cosmic certainty would overwhelm my youthful mind.

Or was it during the process of my daughter's birth when I was propelled along a path that was unexplainable — and I gave birth to the two of us at once? Or was it years later when I first set eyes upon Bob, and knew that we would meet and know one another intimately.

It could also have been the day I purchased *A Course in Miracles* at the Unity Church in West Palm Beach. But by then a pattern of events was evolving in such a way that I could no longer ignore them.

No. I think the event that most significantly identified the onset of this blindwalk was the storm.

PART ONE

THE EAST
AND
AWAKENING

Chapter 1

TWO BEINGS ON A LEAF

 A blindfold can indeed obscure your sight, but cannot make the way itself grow dark. And He who travels with you has the light.

A Course in Miracles

We left the island of Jost Van Dyke, British Virgin Islands, on June 15, 1984 and set sail for the Eastern seaboard of the United States, the entrance to the Chesapeake, to be exact. My husband Bob, our dog, a Schipperke named T.J. Bogart, and I were on our first major ocean cruise without additional crew. We planned to be at sea about 16 days.

We sailed out of the snug, sunny harbor feeling like Sir Francis Drake off on a voyage of discovery. Horizon, our 37-foot, Dutch-built, steel Zeeland Yawl, had just gone through extensive restoration. She looked and sailed like the proud ship she had once been 30 years earlier. Bob and I had spent the better part of six years sandblasting, having her welded throughout and rerigged. When she was finally professionally painted from stem to stern, she looked like a queen, sleek and narrow abeam, ready to tackle the highest of the high seas.

Below deck she was a beauty too, with African mahogany and stained glass windows adorning the joinery. We had fallen in love with this lady at first sight of her in a boathouse near Philadelphia. During the restoration, both in Bayfield, Wisconsin, and later in the U.S. Virgin Islands, I had some doubts about our efforts, but that day I felt only pride.

We were hoisting spanking new North sails and, as the wind caught the mainsail, I grinned with satisfaction. This, I thought, is what life is all about: purity of air, freedom of movement, challenge and risk, excitement and expectation. Joy, pure joy.

On the 16th day, we were within 100 miles of Cape Hatteras. Although we had just experienced 24 hours of near gale winds, the trip overall had been smooth. I daydreamed of our arrival and the anticipation we felt was sweet indeed. We hadn't been stateside in three years. My daydreams were distracted, then obscured, as the winds and sea began to build once again and the skies closed down around us. "How dare there be another storm?" I fumed aloud. Bob radioed the nearest ship whose crew gave us an accurate location to corroborate out sextant readings. We were cer-

tain this storm would be fast upon us, so we grudg-
ingly began to close up the boat and pull back on
our foul weather gear. It was still wet from the earlier gale. We put T.J. down below and hooked
ourselves into our safety harnesses.

Bob and I decided to stand watch together
since he was already exhausted, not having slept
for 24 hours. The seas were building and portended
disaster. We were flying only a single foresail, but
with the increasing force of wind and wave I was
not strong enough to control the tiller. Bob took
over. I felt useless. We braced ourselves, awaiting
our fate.

As the rough seas and wind speed increased
in force, it began to dawn on us — this was a storm
the likes of which we had never experienced in 11
years in inland sea and ocean sailing. Early on we
had learned the Beaufort scale, 12 descriptions
of wave action to estimate wind force. In less than
three hours we had witnessed the wind and sea
build from force five to force eight, gale conditions. We would never choose to be out of harbor
under these conditions but now we had nowhere
to go and no means to get there. We were being
blown towards the middle of forever, and this
thought sent a chilling alarm through my head.

The only good fortune was that, according to
our compass, we were being driven northeasterly

towards Europe and not into the notorious Atlantic graveyard of ships, Cape Hatteras. That would have meant certain death for us all.

By the fifth hour, the face of the sea indicated a full-fledged force 11 storm: winds 72 miles per hour, waves 30 feet or higher. Our boat's mast became an insignificant yardstick.

We had become aliens in a lunatic world of thunderous white foam. When the winds were at full force, the rain and sea spray were blown horizontally. As Horizon skidded down the waves at twice her theoretical maximum speed, she threatened to spin out of control. Thank God she was made of steel!

When the fury of the wind momentarily let up, the monstrous seas again pulsed their warning. They threatened to overrun us each time Horizon plunged through a trough. The boat was pitching wildly. I braced my legs against the opposite cockpit seat. Ships that go down are not blown over, I remembered. They are driven under, without a trace, by the weight of an overtaking wave.

By the eighth hour it was evident there was nothing we could do. We were in open space and the only choices we had were to continue to struggle or let go.

At that time Bob and I had been married for

11 years. We met after each had experienced a divorce. I brought two children, Scott and Tara, into his life and he brought Catherine into mine. I was drawn to him from the moment I saw him. We both felt connected from our first conversation in the faculty lounge on the campus where we both worked. He is a handsome and kind man with a deep integrity at the soul of his being. But in those days he preferred to cover up the pain he felt from significant losses in his life. He was raw in the early years and easily provoked. Never ones to live life simply and easily, Bob and I had a tumultuous beginning in our partnership. We had not been strangers to the storms of human interactions in the name of so-called love.

As I sat braced against the cold, wet steel of the cockpit, I thought of how far we had come in our understanding of one another and how much I wanted to experience it all, including old age and the wisdom and peace it promised. Is it ending so soon? I asked. The thought of death brought fear into my heart. No! dammit, no! It's not fair, I railed against the monstrous storm that was carrying us forward against our wills.

Bob was desperately trying to control the tiller. He was thoroughly exhausted. His yellow slicker was taut against his weakening body. With each surge of wind and wave, gallons of water poured down over his face and torso as he fought to hold the tiller steady against his chest. He looked over at me, his face a paradox of sadness and devotion, and quietly mouthed, "I love you." I had heard these words many times. This time though, he was saying goodbye and warning me of the probable outcome. I murmured, "I love you too." The tears slid down my cheeks for the first time, my eyes burning from the salt and the cold. We were past exhaustion, chilled to the bone and abandoned.

My mind filled with visions of our family, especially our children. If we disappeared without a trace, I thought, their loss would be compounded. There would always be that nagging spark of hope left by the uncertainty of our fate. The tears at that moment were for them.

I suddenly experienced a consciousness, a cosmic connection that can only be described as Holy. In spite of the fact that we faced almost certain death, I felt a vivid, loving link with the universe.

I had felt this magnificent sensation only one other time in my life — at a football game sitting next to my father. The fall colors were at their peak all around the field and the world was alive with warmth and release. We had both been sitting excitedly on the edge of our seats in the end zone when suddenly the whole stadium erupted in cheers. People rose to their feet, all celebrating together. Score one for our team! We won! We won! And standing there filled with raw emotions I felt my spirit merge with all the other beings around us. We were no longer separate selves at a football game. We had become a glorious grand synergy. "We won" had become "we are one."

I looked about me at the surreal scene now engulfing us and I was distinctly aware that Bob and I had chosen this crossroad in our lives. I understood with certainty that no other path could have been possible for us. No other lessons could be learned unless we somehow survived the cosmic lesson of this fearful open space and experienced with absolute clarity the terrifying freedom of letting go. We had become blind to the earthly horizon but were aboard the Horizon in a day out of time. I sucked in my breath as these thoughts pelted me, just as the rain and the sea had been doing for hours. And within me I heard words. They rang like church bells. "Glad tidings," they sang. "Be strong," they cried. "You will make it," they shouted over and over again. And with the force of their message came a deep, calm peace.

I believe, in that instant, in that greater awareness beyond my earth-bound ego — that fearful, controlling, separated part of me — that I saw through the eyes of Truth, felt with the heart of

Truth, and thought with the mind of Truth. Just momentarily. Just for an instant. Eternal Truth.

I shouted to Bob. "Let Horizon handle it. Let's go below!" He looked at me without comprehension. "You're exhausted!" I cried. He nodded silently, his head bent over as if thoroughly beaten down. But suddenly he responded by barking orders.

"Take the tiller! I'll crawl forward and try to get the sail down." I slid to his place at the tiller and we exchanged places. The force of the sea was stronger than I was. If I lost hold, Bob could be thrown overboard.

He struggled towards the bow, dragging his harness line and grasping at the lifeline. When he reached the jib sail, his wet frozen hands somehow managed to release the halyard, letting it fly free. Against odds, the small sail fell to the deck where he left it.

Bob inched his way back towards the stern, crouching all the way. When he tumbled into the cockpit, we immediately made ready to go below. Bob tied the tiller to starboard, pointing Horizon a few degrees into the wind where it held course. The chances of being hit broadside by a wave were now greatly reduced.

"Release your harness," he shouted. "You go first." I slid open the hatchcover and released my safety harness. As I swung my leg over the storm boards, a large wave broke over the entire boat, throwing me sideways. The only thing that saved me from washing overboard was the hatchcover slamming shut, pinning my fingers. Bob cursed with relief.

Once upright, I quickly scrambled below. Bob followed. T.J. did not greet us. He was crouched in a corner of the cabin shaking with fear and ex-haustion.

We secured the hatchcover and stumbled to our bunks in the main cabin. "Let me tie you in," I said to Bob. "I'll stay awake for awhile just to keep an eye on things. He morosely agreed, and stow-ing his raingear in the forepeak, crawled into his berth. I strapped him in with pillows for padding. Then I fumbled to get ahold of T.J. and brought him into my berth.

Horizon continued to pitch and roll fiercely, but I felt somehow more secure below. Bob was fast asleep within minutes. I opened a can of tuna but one bite was all I could swallow before my gagging reflex kicked in. I reached behind me and grabbed the bourbon out of the liquor locker, think-ing the fluid would be easier on my innards. A swig out of the bottle proved me wrong again, as the effects throughout my body were electrical. "Hmm. Adrenaline pumping," I mused aloud to

T.J. The porthole opposite me appeared to be under water. "I give up," I sighed to the universe. "I need some sleep." T.J. and I snuggled in and tied the straps.

We all slept fitfully, awakening from time to time just to see if we were still there. T.J. finally had to pee so badly that we put the line on his harness and inched open the hatchcover, throwing him out into the cockpit. He peed all over a cushion, somehow miraculously still intact on board. Quickly we pulled him back in. The three of us stayed below awaiting our fate for over 27 hours.

When the winds slowed to about 40 miles per hour, we climbed out into the cockpit. Bob managed to get a single sextant sight on the murky sun. We set our 30-year-old storm sail but its senile tissues were immediately torn from the mast. We substituted with a fully reefed mainsail and set a westerly course, knowing we should reach land eventually.

By Bob's sun-sight calculations, we had been borne nearly 180 miles without sails during the past 24 hours, an almost incomprehensible distance. As night fell, we saw the lights of a ship nearby. We called for assistance in pinpointing our latitude and longitude. The captain expressed surprise at hearing from a vessel our size and finding us still afloat. He then corroborated our sextant reading.

Horizon's engine compartment had been filled with more than 300 gallons of sloshing seawater. The paint on the port side of the hull had been literally blasted down to the steel by the storm's force despite the lengthy painting process she had undergone prior to departure. But our amazon of the sea, including her intricate rigging, was intact. We had neglected to tie down our shiny red gas cans however. Knowing they float, we figured they would soon be found and lashed to another deck heading who knows where.

We arrived back in the United States of America on day 20 of our journey, July 4, 1984. The significance of that date is imprinted in my heart.

Chapter 2

INDEPENDENCE DAY

 Our walk of faith must be a daily experience, and our experiences can occur everywhere, in all events. When we are ready to learn of this, the teachers appear, guidance comes our way and we are shown a new way of being.
Principle of Blindwalking

When we realized we needed to sail, not motor, into Cape May, New Jersey, we radioed the Coast Guard to ask for the location of an anchorage. They gave us a bleak outlook on either berths or anchorages due to the holiday crowd. We had gathered something of the sort as we sailed in circles in front of the long break wall entryway surrounded by countless vessels and on shore, people everywhere. Yet this proved to be our fortune as well. One of the many powerboats angling for a better view buzzed up to us and a man shouted, "I've been listening to your transmission on the radio. Welcome back to the U.S. I know where you can anchor once you sail in." He gave us directions to an anchorage right inside the entryway. Thanking him profusely, we started our sail down the rock lined and narrow entryway channel.

It too was jammed with boats coming and going. Apparently other boaters had heard our radio transmission as well for we were accorded a very wide berth. We didn't understand at that time, but realized later that Horizon's paint-scraped hull looked as if it had been in a scrap with a hurricane and we were not to be reckoned with.

We soon were anchored but decided to stay just long enough to pump the storm water from the engine compartment. The boat was second to our concern about getting to shore to call family. Because we were so long overdue, our wish to allay our loved one's fears overshadowed any exhilaration we might have felt about being back in the States.

Pumping the bilge took more than three hours and, although uneventful, became a source of frustration. Work was the last thing we wanted to do. Celebrations were in order on such an auspicious occasion after all! We finally were able to start the engine and weighed anchor only to discover that there was no room in the Marina for us to dock.

As we motored about the harbor we spotted a small waterway south of the main marina and Coast Guard station. We hoped it would offer refuge. There was one other marina on this waterway but it was also full and the creek dead-ended at a low bridge with no further recourse for Horizon. Bob cracked that we were up ship's creek without a paddle — or anchorage.

As we were preparing to turn about, Bob spotted a short, older woman and a younger man standing on a porch watching us with great interest. Their house stood on stilts, as did several of the small, tidy-looking houses in a row along the creek. This couple was within shouting distance so Bob yelled out to them, "Do you know where we can tie up for the night?"

The woman pointed down at the low lying pier next to her house and shouted back, "Sure. Right here."

The tide was running swiftly out of the creek so we coasted rather rapidly toward the dock next to her home. The young man ran down a small flight of stairs to the dock and caught our midships line. Within minutes we were snugged into the pier.

Our host walked over to us and, without formalities, he asked, "Would you like a cold beer?" We both exclaimed, "Yes! Thank you!" He disappeared back up the stairs.

The woman leaned down from her porch and, with what sounded to me like a slight Irish accent said, "I'm off to get some soft-shell crab for dinner. You might as well join us. Make yourself at home. Use the shower," she recommended, "and consider using the guest bed. You look soaked from stem to stern."

We looked up at her in stunned amazement. I managed to mumble, "Uh, would it be okay to use your phone for some credit card calls, too? We need to call our family."

"Of course" she replied tersely, and she was gone. I realized it wasn't her accent that made me think of Ireland, but her appearance. She had qualities of earthiness and elfin-like innocence that I associate with Ireland.

Bob and I looked at each other. We were welcomed home indeed. "Who said there was no room in the inn?" I asked rhetorically to no one in particular. We hugged each other in sweet acknowledgment of our good fortune. I silently said a prayer of gratitude for this precious turn of events. Thanks be to strangers cheerfully giving gifts to strangers in spontaneous and joyful ways.

The young man returned with three cold beers and settled himself on the dock. " I'm Charles," he said, " but prefer the name 'Nick'. And where have you two been?" he asked with a smile.

Thus began a special friendship with Jane Elliott and her shirt-tail relative, Nick. I smiled when I learned that our benefactress was an Elliott, for that is my maternal family name, and Jane was behaving for all the world like a mother hen to us. She just couldn't do enough.

We spent several days at her home. She took us shopping and sightseeing, and to the laundromat with five loads of soggy wash. We all collapsed on the floor in glee when we discovered that Bob inadvertently had grabbed flour out of an unmarked galley container instead of clothes soap. By the time we discovered this, however, all five loads were making paste in the machines.

Horizon and crew visited Jane many times thereafter. Her door was always open as was her heart.

During our first visit, Nick gave Bob a book which I later discovered aboard the boat. He told Bob he was fond of this book. "I'm not sure why," he said, "but I feel you should have it."

Power Through Constructive Thinking, by Emmet Fox became a source of inspiration to me throughout the next year. I read and reread it. Whenever I let the book open to any page for inspiration, it inevitably opened to page 176:

Whoever you are, your true place is calling, calling; and because you really are a spark of the Divine, you will never be content until you answer.

Remember that this call is the call of God, and when God calls you to His Service, He pays all the expenses in whatever kind of coin...money, opportunity, introductions, knowledge, training, freedom, leisure, strength and courage — all will He furnish if you be about His business and not your own.

Your heart's desire is the Voice of God, and that Voice must be obeyed sooner or later.

PART TWO

THE SOUTH
AND
GROWTH

Chapter 3

TRANSITIONS

It may strike some as at least daffy that we continued sailing following the Atlantic adventure. Bob and I tried to discuss the pros and cons rationally, once we were back on dry land, but neither of us could talk about it with any dispassion, so we dropped the subject. It was still such a raw and unnerving encounter that I suspect we both preferred not to relive the memories for a while. I tucked the entire matter into my mental knapsack and hung it out to dry. Without plan or rationale, we were soon back on the Atlantic sailing north to New England.

We were without our loyal friend and crew member, T.J., however, for tragedy had struck. While repainting the boat, we went for a visit to Bob's family in Delaware. T.J. was a wise boat dog but not knowing the dangers of roads, had suddenly run into the street and was killed by a truck. Our grief was profound as he was the third member of a crew that had survived the storm. Bob's brother, Jim, an animal lover too, dug a deep hole in the back yard of their home and helped us wrap T.J. in his blanket and lay him to rest in the earth. The next day a small white cross appeared over the gravesite.

To honor T.J., we ended our ship's log with his death and began a new logbook, thus symbolizing a significant change in the journey. The gap left by T.J.'s death remained though, and we spoke little of it.

The sail along the southern New England coast is rivaled in our memory only by the prior Caribbean portion of our adventure. We spent time in such intriguing locales as Sandy Hook, New York Harbor, the East river and a lengthy sojourn at City Island, the entrance to Long Island Sound. Our new Schipperke joined us there.

It had been a difficult decision to replace T.J. so soon. We felt somehow disloyal. But Bob's sister Nancy had been so insistent about it that she personally located a Schipperke pup in Virginia. "He has a white spot on his chest," she said excitedly over the phone. "so he's imperfect and can't be bred. He's half price."

The fat little pup emerged from his carrier at La Guardia airport the next week. He was the shape of a baked-potato on short, spindly legs, but black and fuzzy with a fox-like head and a ruff around his neck. There were raw circles around both eyes and on his nose which the breeder had explained were due to fly bites. The white spot was noticeable even in the dim lighting of the freight terminal. "He looks like a cross between a bear cub and a fox!" I exclaimed.

Bob was obviously disappointed. T.J. had been a perfect specimen of Schipperke, and in no way did this pup resemble T.J. "Hey, let's hear it for the underdog," I muttered, swooping the pup up into my arms.

It was Bob, however, who came up with the perfect name: Charley Noble. It's a nautical term for a blackened galley stovepipe on a boat. It was also Bob who promptly dove overboard in the Stanford, Connecticut, harbor when Charley fell into the drink.

Seems Charley hadn't yet recognized the pre-cariousness of his new home. He was sniffing about Horizon's deck his first day under sail and decided to explore outside one of the stantions guarding the edge of the deck. I was at the helm and seeing the black blur plop into the water, I yelled out "It's Charley. He's overboard!"

Bob turned, surveyed the scene and dove overboard too. Both Bob and Charley were im-mediately in the wake of the boat, each paddling mightily in the water. It took me three attempts at figure-eights, the standard rescue maneuver, to get Horizon in position for a pickup. By that time two men in a small fishing boat had motored over within saving distance as well.

As the soggy twosome hoisted themselves back onto the deck, the men broke into a round of applause and one yelled, "Great job. Do it again!"

Bob said later that he hadn't trusted Charley's swimming ability but admitted that Charley had been swimming perfectly. We could sense the new crew was beginning to gel.

Bob's daughter, Catherine, came to visit us, fresh from a summer as an exchange student in Spain, and we sailed up the coast of Connecticut. We particularly relished Mystic where we berthed and explored nautical history at Mystic Seaport for two beautiful days.

Bob, Charley and I continued on to Massachusetts, Rhode Island and such delightful spots as Martha's Vineyard, Nantucket, Cuttyhunk and Block Island. We met fellow sailors everywhere and were treated with care and concern by locals in all ports of call.

Our journey in New England was cut short by a phone conversation with Bob's mom, Jean. We were exploring Block Island with friends, Ivy and

Lorna, whose boat was moored next to ours and had no intentions of leaving any time soon.

But Jean's voice was strained when she answered the phone that day. Her first words were, "Did the Coast Guard find you?"

"No," I replied. "Just calling to check in. What's wrong?"

Her voice quavered as she said, "Nancy has been diagnosed with cancer — lung cancer and a possible brain tumor. She began to cry.

We left Block Island the next morning and three days later were docked at Jane Elliott's in Cape May. We borrowed a car to join the family in Delaware for the first of what became many trips from our permanent anchorage in Solomon's Island, Maryland, to Nancy's side. Six months later she was gone.

She had long been like a sister to me as has Isabel, my other sister-in-law. As an only child I cherished these two women. Losing one of them was painful. But for Bob and his family it was doubly so. They were experiencing the loss of a child and sibling for the second time. It occurred to us as we reminisced about her one evening that our sailing adventure was dishing out major lessons in life and death: first the storm, then T.J., now Nancy.

That winter we received a letter from a boat

broker reminding us of our earlier expressed interest in a boat named Sopris. We had seen pic-
tures of this one-of-a-kind work of art at the annual wooden boat show when we were visiting
Newport, Rhode Island. Jim Payne's letter served
as a reminder of the boat's intrigue for us. She is a
40-foot double-ended cutter, entirely hand crafted
of wood. She took six years from design to launch,
at the loving hands of Maine boat builder, David
Nutt.

Horizon had become a symbol of strength and
spirit in our minds and hearts. But living aboard
Horizon had not been easy despite her impressive
length since she was only ten foot abeam. And
she had little capacity for drinking water, fuel and
storage, not to mention sleeping space — if one
liked sleeping next to one's mate, which Bob and
I do. Having lived on Horizon for a year, these features tended to magnify in significance, and we
were feeling the effects.

We talked of Sopris on many occasions but
then felt disloyal, as if Horizon could hear us and
would find us ungrateful. We finally decided that a
trip to Maine by plane would be a lark and we
would simply stop by Boothbay Harbor to see
Sopris as a part of the Maine pilgrimage. No other
plans but those, we kept reminding ourselves
sternly. So during a mid-winter break from odd

jobs in Solomon's Island and our monthly visits to Delaware, we flew north to Boothbay Harbor.

We were hooked the minute we stepped aboard this wondrous boat. David, who had crafted her for himself, was now releasing her after several years of intimate work and exhilarating sailing. She was broad beamed, impressively strong, beautiful to look upon and a live aboard's dream. Her cabins were luxurious and she had a double berth in the aft cabin. Refrigeration, ice cubes, huge storage tanks, a wheel, and a feeling of serenity spoke seductively to us. But most of our savings would have to go towards her purchase. We returned to Horizon in a quandary.

After much soul searching, we devised a plan to buy and charter Sopris in the Chesapeake, thus rationalizing our need for her. Once we made this decision, we moved full steam ahead to make it a reality. It wasn't until the day we put a for-sale sign on Horizon that I caught myself wondering how we could ever have done such a thing. I spent a long time below on Horizon that day, reliving the storm and other adventures and shedding some necessary tears.

Joel, a fellow from Solomon's Island, offered to buy Horizon. He seemed to be so enamored of her that we decided to let him buy her with little down and a contract for deed.

Soon after this decision was made, another offer for full payment came and we felt obligated to take it. "It will assist in the purchase of Sopris," we argued with Joel. He countered by saying "You guys made a promise. You said she was mine."

Against good sense, we felt ethically bound to Joel. A ten year contract was signed and Horizon was Joel's, at least on paper. Things were working out smoothly and we excitedly planned our sail aboard Sopris from Maine to the Chesapeake where she would become our new home.

Chapter 4

AGNES OF GOD

 When you meet anyone, remember it is a holy encounter.

A Course in Miracles

In retrospect many of the events on Solomon's Island were clearly significant. But we took little notice at the time. Jobs, free berths for Horizon, the buying of Sopris, the sale of Horizon, visits with Scott and Catherine and trips to Delaware were all manifesting and unfolding in an unrecognized order. Our charter business, Rightside Yachtworks, was finally operational and old sailing friends were gliding back into the harbor for joyful reunions. But these events, although greatly appreciated, were mostly taken for granted.

There was one experience however, that finally caused us to pause and reassess the serendipity that was occurring in our lives. Who would have thought that our teacher would be a car?

We had decided in the spring that we needed some cheap means of ground transportation. Our answer appeared the next day. We were visited by a local couple who had heard we were anchored in Solomon's and living aboard our boat. The man shared Bob's background in biology and they both shared our love of sailboats. During an evening together I mentioned our need for a car. He smiled and said, "We have one for sale. Her name is Agnes."

They'd had Agnes for years and swore by her. "She's for sale for the grand sum of $300.00," he said. Without hesitating Bob replied, "Sold. We'll pick her up in the morning." I looked at Bob and smiled.

The next day we walked over to their home and, upon entering the yard, were greeted with the sight of a spiffy looking sedan and a disreputable looking junker. I swallowed and said, "Guess which one is ours." Bob sighed. "Agnes, huh?" I mumbled, thinking of the movie title. "I suspect she'll be known as 'Agnes of God' because I don't see how in the world she can even move without Divine Intervention."

We parted with our $300.00 and drove Agnes back to the boat landing. She turned out to be one of the most rewarding purchases we have ever made. Agnes performed admirably, allowing us to charter our boat, provision with ease, and drive to community events we normally might have had to forgo. We also were able to continue our trips to Delaware, no minor feat for someone of Agnes's age. It became routine as we rolled into Jim's driveway in Wilmington, to be met with either a round of applause or lots of hoots and hollers in observance of another successful trip.

We readied to leave the Chesapeake by fall. We wanted to continue our odyssey further south and soon would need jobs since our money was fast running out. This was the time to make our move.

With strong feelings of genuine affection we put a for-sale sign in Agnes' window. The asking price: $250. Nothing happened. We lowered the price to $150. Still no offers. We dropped the price to $50. Still no takers.

With only a week left in the Chesapeake, Agnes' new owner appeared. I was on my way to a little town up the road for a haircut. About a half-mile from town, Agnes suddenly seemed to explode. The engine shifted position; an engine mount had broken. The gas tank had also sprung a leak but did not catch fire, a blessing since I was fully aware of the danger at that moment. I inched into town and parked in a space away from buildings, scrambling out as quickly as I could.

My feet had barely hit the pavement when a lad of about 15 came running up to me shouting, "Boy, lady, have you ever got problems!" I looked at him and said, "Yup. Want to buy a car?"

"How much?" he asked. "One dollar," I said. "You've got a deal, lady," he grinned. I filled out the registration card, he handed me $1.00 and I still made my hair appointment.

It seems Agnes had all along understood The Four Immutable Principles of Events, noted by Harrison Owen, my friend and colleague from Maryland:

"Whenever it starts is the right time (and she did), whoever is there is the right people (and they were), whatever happens is the only thing that could happen (so be it), and when it's over, it's over." (and boy - was it ever).

Agnes of God's presence in our lives has become a milepost for me. Call the events of her life with us serendipity or coincidence, whichever. She symbolizes a powerful lesson in manifestation of needs. She is a lesson in simplicity, a lesson in allowing things to unfold in unfamiliar ways, and surely, in the necessity of detaching ourselves from the outcome. Who but the Universe, could have planned it better? I hope it's gone as well for the lad who bought her.

Chapter 5

ON OUR WAY TO WHERE?

 *The simplest questions are the most profound.
Where were you born? Where is your home?
Where are you going? What are you doing?
Think about these once in a while, and watch
your answers change.*

Richard Bach

By Thanksgiving week we were well down the Inland Waterway and staying at Stuart, Florida. We had headed there to attend the gathering of the Seven Seas Boating Association.

Our first day on arrival we rowed the dingy ashore to join the throng of strangers milling about at the gathering. As we came around the corner of a building, Bob and I were commenting on the difficulties of getting to know people when I ran smack into a handsome, greying stranger who was dashing around the corner the other way. Having collided, we exchanged concerns and then giggles which led to other talk. Ken, finding we were live aboards, offered us the use of his car to post some letters. After that we agreed to meet for lunch.

Ken and his wife were also live aboards, inhabiting a sailboat docked on Jupiter Island in Tequesta, just a short distance down the Inland Waterway. Ken leaned across the table and said spontaneously, "Pull into the marina on Jupiter Island, meet my wife Dana, and join us for dinner when you sail by."

"Sounds like a wonderful idea," I chirped. Bob added, "What about the possibility of employment in Palm Beach County?"

Ken was encouraging. "There are 37 municipalities in that county," he said, "And a growth rate not to be believed. You should have no trouble whatsoever."

Several days later we pulled into the Jupiter Island marina to say hello to Ken and Dana. Within a day we were surrounded by friendly, outgoing, supportive folks who lived aboard various sailboats and luxurious motor yachts. This was our new home, we decided, so we signed a lease, installed a phone, and became respectable residents of Palm Beach County.

I remember some of our new-found friends scoffing at us for trying to land a job under these fly-by-night circumstances. I said I disagreed and would have a job in no time.

Much to even my own surprise, I had two job offers within thirty days. The second offer was a perfect fit and paid a reasonable salary. I would be located on the campus of Palm Beach Community College as Director of the Institute of Government within the Continuing Education department. I had no idea what a significant role this job would play in my future, but I was more than ready to tackle job responsibilities once again.

Bob was not as fortunate as individuals with Ph.D.'s are harder to place. Consequently he took several odd jobs and one very unsatisfactory professional job while we were in Florida. But as we would later learn, this too played a role in future developments.

We spent several wonderful months at this marina and developed dear and warm friendships. A pool and a short path to the ocean were among the benefits, and many weekends routinely included exploring this splendid area and relaxing with friends. We became particularly close to our dock neighbors, Steve and LuAnn, and cooked up all sorts of parties and other excuses for fun with these two and the other "yachties."

Reconnecting with our family was now also possible. Scott had visited us in Maryland and Delaware and now Catherine came for Christmas and Tara for Easter. Bob's mother was there as well from time to time. It felt like reentry into civilization in many ways, which I welcomed after a-year-and-a-half of sailing.

Throughout this sojourn, Charley Noble survived more bouts with death than any being we
had ever known. His legs got caught in the web-
bing of a lift bridge as he jumped ship and ran
after our car one day. A policeman found him and
took him to headquarters where we picked Charley up after many frantic phone calls. Our pooch
traversed some of the busiest streets in West Palm
Beach without a scratch. He fell overboard while
we were at work and found himself surrounded by
walls of concrete. Someone finally grabbed him
in the nick of time. He also fell overboard with his
collar and rope on, and hung by his neck 'til found
by another marina resident. We swore that Charley had a guardian angel. And we were always
immensely grateful, as Charley had become a
great joy to both of us. But he was also a handful!

Bob came home with an advertisement from
a local "what's happening" magazine one day
while in Tequesta. He pointed to an ad which described a meditation group led by a woman who
lived near the marina. "Thought you might be interested in this," he said. I was.

I called the office number in the ad and was
told by a voice at the other end that it would be
fine for me to attend. When I walked up to a
townhouse the following week I was greeted at the
door by a most unusual woman in a long flowing

gown. She looked at me quizzically but invited me in. Shortly afterwards, others came and we had a very low key but pleasant meditation session in her home.

When I returned the next week, she greeted me at the door with a chuckle and said, "Oh yes, come on in. You're one of us." It turned out that the magazine was outdated, the information I had received was inaccurate and the group had been closed to any new member for quite some time. She explained that they had proceeded very cautiously at the last session, not knowing who I was.

"How do you know for certain that I'm okay? That I'm one of you?" I asked.

"Because I am a psychic," she said. "It's my business to know." This was new and intriguing news.

This was my first experience with a psychic. I gained respect for her and all of the people who met with her each week. We shared quietly in meditations, letting-go rituals and discussion of issues in each of our lives. Often she would give advice or information to one or more of us and I found her intuitive talents uncanny in both candor and accuracy.

Over coffee one night, members of the group told me about the Unity Church of West Palm Beach. Many of them were regular attendees. As I found out later, the link to the next step in the journey had now been established.

Meanwhile things were getting a little hairy aboard Sopris. Bob was disgruntled about lack of work, and I felt put upon by his negative moods. Boats tend to get smaller as tempers start to flare. Especially boats that are not actively sailing somewhere.

The hairiness escalated one night over spaghetti dinner. I was eating hurriedly in order to make a meeting with the group and an argument ensued over my lack of consideration for Bob's feelings in my haste to get going. I countered with my usual aplomb, "You're just jealous of this group."

His response was to lift up his plate and toss the spaghetti into the air, draping the interior of Sopris in dripping wet sauce and noodles. I looked at him in astonishment, paused to consider this, and tossed my plate of spaghetti up into the air, thus adding to the mess. I promptly departed from the salon for my meeting.

Before heading back to the boat, I asked our group leader if she had any insights on when we might expect a break from the present doldrums. She replied, "You've got a long way to go, my friend, a long way to go."

I arrived back on Sopris to find Bob in bed

and Charley on clean-up detail all by himself. He was up on the table vainly trying to get to the noodles still stuck to the cabin roof. "A long, long way to go," I muttered, as I rolled up my shirt sleeves to begin the cleanup.

Chapter 6

SEEKING UNITY

 This world is a school. That and nothing more. When we learn that God is all that is and thought is power, we then remember who we truly are. When we remember who we truly are, Children of God, we are able to let go of our fear and return to a state of love.
                                    Images from a dream, 1994

We stayed on Jupiter Island for several months, but by summer of 1986 Bob had located a job in West Palm Beach. A move closer to both our work sites was imperative. We located a marina directly across from Palm Beach, in the heart of West Palm Beach, and made our move. With sadness, we left the gang at Jupiter Island, but soon made new friends with Art and JB. They approached life eagerly and shared our thirst for knowledge through books and other adventures. The four of us had many a wild conversation over dinner aboard Wu Wie or Sopris.

We decided to have boat cushions made for Sopris, and contacted a fellow at the marina who dealt in canvas. He came to measure the boat. In addition to discussing cushions, I discovered that he attended Unity Church.

"It's just five blocks south of the marina," he said. "I thoroughly enjoy the Rosencranzes, the couple who are the ministers. I think you will too. They're innovative and deeply spiritual. And the church itself is filled with opportunities for people of all ages." I remembered the group in Tequesta speaking of this same church and thought, how peculiar; here we are now living only five blocks away.

I decided to attend the following Sunday. This was a departure from the past for I had given up organized religion some years previously. I was reluctant to attend because I often witnessed hypocrisy within the church community. I also had difficulty understanding traditional interpretations of both the Bible and the life of Jesus. The mysticism escaped me. But the people in the meditation group had introduced me to a different level of mysticism and meditation and I was ready to pursue anything that would further this understanding.

I stood admiring the church building. It felt solid and lofty at the same time. In contrast, when I entered the building, I found the sanctuary to be more like an auditorium. It seated well over 200 people and there was a stage with a podium and some chairs. It felt refreshing in its simplicity. (This was never so underscored as at Christmas time when the <u>only</u> decoration was a lighted Christmas tree design about two feet high shining from the front of the podium.)

When I returned to the boat I was bursting with excitement. I cornered Bob over lunch and shared with him. "In contrast to the starkness of the sanctuary, there's a palpable peace and a feeling of belonging that truly calls to me. I haven't felt this way about a church for a long time. The room feels safe, the people feel connected, the ministers are joyful and emphasize the idea of service. There's genuine laughter, Bob. And I experienced a feeling of grace in the silences. They actually meditate and when they do, you can feel Divinity in the room. It's the opposite of the past where prayer has been either rote, or written in the bulletin or done by the minister for all those seated below. Why don't you come with me next Sunday?"

Bob looked at me and said succinctly, "I'm happy for you, Diane. But you know how I feel about organized religion. No thanks."

I attended Unity faithfully from then on and discovered that the foundation for many of the sermons was something known as "*A Course In Miracles*." I was intrigued by these teachings and how they related to our daily lives. I felt an excite-

ment as each Sunday drew near and eagerly an-
ticipated the journey down Flagler Drive to learn
more about a life filled with miracles.

Chapter 7

VOICES

 We have to do it alone. Our path is a personal journey and, although others may be there to assist, it is truly between us and the Holy Spirit. We are challenged to listen to our natural inner wisdom. Therefore we are wise to learn to trust our Higher Self first and foremost.

Principle of Blindwalking

I was browsing in Rainbow Bridge, a bookstore in downtown West Palm Beach one Saturday. Wandering amidst books, incense and soft music, thoroughly enjoying myself, I heard a voice, a distinct voice which said "You have to do it alone." Expecting to see the person I had overheard, I swung abruptly around. No one was there. The owner was behind the counter reading. The only other customer was far down the aisle with her back to me.

I turned back to the shelf, pretending that it hadn't happened. But I knew that I had heard a voice. Crazy people hear voices, I thought. I'm not about to become crazy! I picked up a book and began thumbing through it. But try as I might, I couldn't get my mind off this strange occurrence.

Nothing like this had ever happened in my life, and were it not for the distinctness of the voice and the clarity of the message, I would have shrugged it off as my imagination. But there was no mistaking this. I had heard a voice. I closed my eyes and shuddered. What is happening to me, I thought fearfully. I felt momentary anger at the voice and the bookstore for disturbing my peace. Bookstore music played in the background while the clock above me ticked in syncopation with the music. They sounded bizarre to my addled brain, not melodic. "Best to leave now," I mumbled to myself.

I hurriedly purchased the paperback I was holding, feeling an obligation to the fellow behind the counter, and headed out the door. When I glanced down at my purchase, I found I had grabbed a book about the famous psychic, Edgar Cayce.

All the way back to the marina I pondered the words. By the time I reached Sopris I was convinced that I had indeed heard some kind of message. I did not feel crazy. But what to make of it? What did it mean?

"You have to do it alone." Why me? Why now?

In the turmoil of my mind I concluded the worst possible: Bob was going to die and I would be left bereft! My stomach churned. What else could such a strange message mean except that I was destined to become a widow, and soon it seemed. I was confused. And afraid for Bob, for myself, for us, for everything.

I tried to forget I had ever heard these words. But I did not forget the message, or the experience. It felt like what a friend once referred to as a Cosmic Boot. The universe was playing "change games" with my head.

Chapter 8

ENDINGS, EMPTINESS AND
BEGINNINGS

 However you have learned to deal with them, endings are the first phase of transition. The second phase is a time of lostness and emptiness before "life" resumes an intelligible pattern and direction, while the third phase is that of beginning anew.

William Bridges

Shortly after the first of the year, we experienced another Cosmic Boot. I picked up Bob at South Florida Water Management District on a sunny Friday afternoon. He had been employed there for six months, and was trying valiantly to make use of his experience as an ecologist. The sailing journey had added to his savvy and he was stronger than ever in his ethical approach to the planet. He cared deeply about whatever environs he inhabited and served, including South Florida.

As we headed back to the marina, I asked how his day had gone. He glanced at me and said wryly, "Not so good. I got a pink slip."

He had been fired! With no warning and for no valid reason that we could see. But he had been a new hire and on probation and it appeared he had little recourse.

I was shocked and angry and frantically began forecasting our impending financial ruin. In five minutes I had us flat broke. "My God, how will we make it on one salary?" I anguished.

We didn't realize it then but we were being introduced to cosmic justice. Since then we have learned that there is a Divine Force that does not punish but uses all events as positive lessons — if we are but willing to be open to them. These lessons were unfolding without our knowledge however, and we were being forced to walk the road blindly.

Finally something stopped my ranting. We sat in silence for a few miles. Then I managed to say, "Well, there may be some reason that you were fired. Let's let it go, head back to the boat and talk. Who knows what may happen next."

I didn't need to make it worse for him. We both knew that vacating this job was also a relief to him in many ways since he had felt professionally compromised all along.

After an hour or so we were feeling much better. We had decided that we would need to find a less expensive marina. Bob knew of one. "It's not West Palm Beach by a long shot," he said, "but it will save us money." Sounded good to me.

The phone rang. It was Chris and Hilda calling from London where they had recently flown after visiting us in Florida.

Chris and Hilda are old friends from Bayfield, Wisconsin, where we had lived and worked for seven years. They had visited us at many of our locales in the journey since our leave-taking from Bayfield aboard Horizon in 1981. We had left the town dock of this picturesque village in the spring-time right after Scott's graduation from high school, setting sail for the U.S. Virgin Islands, new jobs and a whole new lifestyle.

Their voices once again reminded me of the town and townspeople we loved so well. I recalled the throng of people waving at us as we tearfully pulled away from the dock. I was holding a huge gift package of locally produced Trinko sausages and beef jerky in my arms as if it was a bouquet and wondering if the tears were for the ache in my heart or the excitement of the horizons that lay ahead for us.

Hilda now said that she and Chris had just called Bayfield. "Pat Miller is looking for you," she said. Pat was superintendent of the Apostle Islands National Lakeshore and had been Bob's boss when we lived there.

"Maybe he wants to offer Bob his old job back!" Hilda kidded. We brought each other up to date, and Bob promised to call Pat.

Pat said, "I was looking for you because I'm

on my way to Florida and wanted to have dinner with you." When Bob told Pat about losing his job, Pat laughed and said, "As a matter of fact, your old job as Park Ecologist is opening up again come summer. Why don't you apply?" When Bob hung up the phone he stared at me and said, "There's a job opening back in Bayfield."

Two weeks later when Pat arrived, he again encouraged Bob to reapply for the job. Bob had vacated this post so we could live and work in the Virgin Islands. When Bob was out of the room Pat said, "He stands every chance of being selected. How would you feel about returning to Bayfield?"

Without admitting it, I had not thought much about a life back in rural America. Nor had I considered what I would find for employment in an area with few professional positions I could fill. I told Pat that I would be excited about the prospect. But deep down I was confused. What was this all about?

Chapter 9

THE PATHWAY OPENS

 The easy path is not conducive to blindwalking. For we must enter the abyss of open space before we can mourn the past and imagine the new. Old gives way to the new as we make room in our lives and ourselves for the possible. We may have been socialized to expect shortcuts and fast fixes but the journey is step by step and stage by stage until we can bless the entire spectrum before us.

Principle of Blindwalking

The next day Bob and I sat under the green canvas awning over our cockpit and made a list. One page for all of the advantages of the job opening in Bayfield: the continuation of benefits through federal reemployment; the return to a place we both loved; closer proximity to our children; a job that Bob would enjoy, his future secure and his wages significant once again; and renewal of old and dear friendships. Then the list of disadvantages: Our sailing days would be over, for we would have to move ashore; we would leave the warm climate of Florida; I would leave my job at the college, work that I loved; I would leave Unity Church; there would be few if any jobs for me back in Wisconsin. I began to feel a sense of foreboding.

It was time for me to rethink things for myself. Sopris' gleaming wood womb called to me, so I went below to be alone in the midst of her peacefulness. I sat at the galley table surrounded by her beauty and wrote and made drawings of my confusion and fears. I explored my concerns about work and acknowledged my excitement about returning. Finally I asked, "what would I do once we were back?" Immediately the words from the bookstore echoed in my head.

"You have to do it alone."

But what was "it" and how will I do it alone?

Then another thought reminded me of a goal I had set for myself several years earlier. That goal was to someday be an independent consultant, giving seminars and consulting in management, supervision and organizational development.

I thought about the past year-and-a-half as Director of the Institute of Government and the diverse education this job afforded me. The working relationship I had with O.H., the Dean of Continuing Education had been filled with lessons and successes. I realized that my employment path had served me well over the years and the Institute job seemed to be capping off these experiences. I was working with and observing some of the best consultants and trainers in Florida. Former graduate work in psychology, theater, educational psychology and communications would also prove to be valuable foundations — if I had the courage to pursue this dream.

I spent two more hours visioning the possibilities and finally felt, in a deeply intuitive way, that I had just unraveled the mystery of the bookstore.

Bob wasn't going to die. We were both going to live! And I was going to birth my own business back in Bayfield, Wisconsin, fulfilling a dream of many years.

And I was going to do it all alone.

I literally flew out of the boat and raced down the dock to find Bob. I nearly collided with the canvas maker, who was pedaling past our dock on his bicycle. I was so excited that I babbled the entire story to him including the voice in the bookstore, the phone call after Bob lost his job, and the decision I had just reached about our possible move to Bayfield.

He smiled and calmly said, "Diane, I didn't come to your boat to make cushions for you. It's obvious I came to tell you about Unity Church and the church has talked to you about *A Course In Miracles*. And now you're experiencing voices and miracles and isn't that just wonderful!"

I looked him fully in the face and realized that he understood exactly. No further explanation needed. We joined in spontaneous and joyful laughter.

Shortly thereafter, Bob and I moved to the Riviera Beach Marina. Bob was offered his federal job back and accepted it. We began making plans to leave Florida and sail Sopris home to Bayfield.

The last time I attended the Unity Church was a most emotional day. I dreaded the leave-taking. This church had resurrected my passion for service and redirected my journey towards God. Faith was a concept that meant more to me now than I had ever thought possible. Metaphysics wasn't just a word in a book anymore. It was a practical path of healing. And my journey had been made richer by far by just being in the company of those who gathered on Sundays to explore truth. I knew few people by name, yet I felt a kinship that crossed physical boundaries. What would I do when I returned to Northern Wisconsin? What would take its place?

The service ended with the singing of "Let There Be Peace on Earth." As we sang, arm in arm, tears rolled down my cheeks and I prayed that by walking blindly into an uncertain future without benefit of this sanctuary, I could still be a part of the Grace that flowed so freely and the

Love that bound us all in community.

As we left the sanctuary, I walked over to the counter of the bookstore, looked down, and there on the shelf was the three volume set of books called *A Course In Miracles*. All these months I had been hearing about these books and yet had never laid eyes on them before. Suddenly it was clear: These teachings were directly available to me. I didn't need someone else to interpret the mysteries that lay within these pages. I could experience it for myself.

I said with great certainty to the woman behind the counter, "I'll take those." Bob will think I'm nuts, I thought, but I didn't care nearly as much about being nuts this time as I did about carrying these books with me into whatever lay ahead.

As I walked out of the church the sun blinded me. I was reminded of the line from the song, *Suzanne*: " The sun came down like honey..." for the heat and brilliance of the day felt like sweetness drenching my body and my mind. I knew that I had what I came to Unity for. Sitting in my arms were magnificent books and they, too, would make the journey back to Wisconsin. For the first time since the storm, I experienced the certainty of Spirit within telling me that it was unfolding in safety and exactly as it must.

On July 2, 1987, Sopris entered Bayfield Harbor, captain and first mate having come full circle after six and one-half years, and exactly three years after the storm. Bob, Charley Noble, myself, and Bob's brother, Jim who had joined us in Tonawonda, New York, were aboard. It was six a.m. A glorious sunrise illuminated and warmed the colorful village nestled against the south shore of Lake Superior.

We were broke. Until Bob's job became full-time in four months, we had the promise of his part-time pay between us. We had only minuscule equity in the boat with which to buy a house. What would have been our down-payment had disappeared into the boat in the form of a new transmission. The old transmission had given out in the Erie Canal. But we were safe, we were blessed and we were home.

PART THREE

THE NORTH
AND
CLARITY

Chapter 10

OLD GIVES WAY TO NEW

 There is no order of difficulty in miracles.
A Course in Miracles

The vision I had of my new office space was a front bedroom with a lake view on the second floor of a white house. We refinanced the boat and began our search.

While driving around town with our realtor one day, we drove by a green house with one of Donna's own lawn signs, but we didn't stop. Donna said, "Knowing your taste, I don't think you'd be interested in that one. It needs a great deal of work." We reminded her that paupers didn't always get their pick.

She was right. It took a lot of imagination, too. But the price fit our meager down payment, the size was perfect, and the yard and the view were outstanding. Our old friend, the Bayfield ravine, was in the back yard.

We had lived above the banks of this ravine in our first Bayfield home and knew its spirit, the lush greenery and paths that wound for miles along its steep sides. There had always been a mystery and a comfort about this ravine, for us as well as our children.

The old iron bridge, long off limits to cars, was two houses away from these back steps as well, still holding its own so town folk and tourists could walk from one side of the ravine to the other. One could hurry across and easily miss the mystic beauty that lay beneath this bridge. I had usually chosen to stay awhile. You can see the Great Lake in the distance. Our dreams of sailing were nurtured while lingering there and gazing at the fresh water of this lake — superior to all other lakes.

This historic bridge also connected directly to the first property we owned in Bayfield. Scott, at age 16, probably while trying to impress his friends, had hung out over the side of this iron truss about 100 feet above the ground to loosen his caught kite string. I could laugh about it now, realizing that this dangerous antic was a prelude to his present passion for mountain climbing.

Perhaps it was symbolic as well that we would now be across the bridge on the other side of the ravine from where we had started. Was this bridge a reminder of Thomas Wolf's caution that you can't go home again? Or was it as T.S. Elliot says, that you go home again and know the place for the first time?

These thoughts convinced me that we should take a chance at this old house on the hill if only for these connections we felt to the surroundings. Bob felt a kinship with the house itself. He talked excitedly about the potential he saw, despite the "remuddeling" that had occurred. The second floor bedroom was just as I had envisioned. The entire house had a view of the downtown, the harbor, the ferryboat to Madeleine Island and the cold clear water of the lake. So what if the house was green. We could paint it.

Thus it was that we entered into one of the major transformation challenges of our 15 years together. Our house on the ravine became a labor of love and an opportunity to continue our co-creative endeavors. This venture was as filled with highs and lows as had been our sailing adventure. And like sailing, we were given space for personal and interpersonal transformations as well.

The day we moved ashore, we went to the local flea market and purchased a beat-up kitchen table and two wooden chairs. We borrowed a four-poster bed, a couch and an easy chair. A few days later I passed by an antique store. There in the back room was a simple old desk. I bought it on the spot, along with a small desk chair.

I placed the desk and chair in the upstairs front bedroom with the peach walls and the peach shag carpet, plugged in a phone and declared myself in business. I called my business Brander and Associates. I had no idea who my associates would be.

About a week later Bob returned from a management seminar grinning smugly. He had mentioned to the seminar leader that I, too, led seminars in management. The leader happened to be looking for someone to add to a continuing education faculty at the University of North Dakota, and asked Bob to have me call him. Bob-the-Scientist saw this as a lucky break, but deep down I think he resonated to the serendipity of it all. For he had once again served as an agent in the blindwalk, thus allowing these events to unfold as needed.

Within another week I had interviewed with this gentleman and was selected to do seminars. This university relationship became the backbone of Brander and Associates for the first two years of its existence. Without it I may have been forced to abandon my plans.

I was learning that when God is in charge, wonders are everyday practical occurrences. It appears that the extraordinary is in fact, ordinary. What we often take to be just a coincidence or a miracle can become the daily foundation of our journey.

I now believe we are continually being asked to stretch ourselves and understand that miracles are normal everyday gifts of Truth. We need only be willing to buy into this. But that may, in fact, be harder than one thinks. For it means giving *everything* over to God.

Chapter 11

THE COURSE AND THE MESSAGES

 All miracles mean life, and God is the Giver of life. His Voice will direct you very specifically. You will be told all you need to know.
A Course in Miracles

As we settled into the routine of living ashore again and throwing ourselves into the business of business, I continued to study *A Course in Miracles.* Before I could seriously undertake this endeavor however, I had to come to terms with the male-oriented language in these books. When I began to accept that we are not body but spirit, I was able to see male pronouns as ultimately irrelevant to the content, and primarily a product of the limitations of our language. I also have for some years leaned towards a belief in reincarnation, and if that is indeed so, we have all been both sexes. With these thoughts in mind, I moved beyond this problem.

The course is divided into three books: a text, a workbook which is designed as a daily lesson for one full year, and a teacher's manual. I concentrated on doing a lesson each day in the workbook. I also read the text as I studied the lessons, building a firmer foundation for understanding this new way of perceiving the world.

This vehicle for enlightenment was showing me a better way. The trick, however, is integrating the messages of the course into everything that occurs in one's life, with no exceptions. It is a challenge I continue to spend my days practicing and perfecting.

One day in early fall of 1987, I was seated at the kitchen table pondering the day's lesson and the miracle of these books' existence. I recalled the story of the Course and began thinking about Helen Schucman, the scribe for the Course during the seven years of its writing from 1965 to 1972. She and Bill Thetford were not likely candidates for such an assignment as this, according to Robert Skutch in his book, *Journey Without Distance*. Helen worked as a medical psychologist with Bill at Columbia University's College of Physicians and Surgeons in New York City. She was Jewish and a professed atheist. Kenneth Wapnick, in his definitive biography of Helen entitled *Absence From Felicity* states, however, that she was a spiritual pilgrim most of her life. He shares that Bill was her superior who became a key supporter for her when the voice within began in earnest. Bill was evidently often more comfortable with this mystic phenomenon than was she, even though she was the actual recipient of "The Voice." He encouraged her by promising to record her inner dictation daily, if she would listen and take notes in shorthand. The first words of the text that she had heard, states Wapnick, were "This is a course in miracles. Please take notes." She knew already that this was the voice of Jesus.

Later she had asked why she had been chosen for such an assignment. As Wapnick verifies, she writes, "I'm not even religious...I'm just about as poor a choice as You could make."

The voice responds, "On the contrary... you are an excellent choice and for a very simple reason. You will do it." I found this answer fascinating in its simplicity.

The possibility occurred to me that, if Helen had such a strong gift for clearly hearing the Jesus voice or a "Voice for God," that a voice was available to everyone in some form or experience unique to each of us.

Wapnick confirms that Helen had heard and simply written down what she heard. She called it a kind of inner dictation. She explained that it occurred in a state of perfect awareness and was in no way automatic.

I decided to try it. I picked up the small phone pad with barely enough room to transcribe more than one sentence on it, and carefully set it in front of me. I glanced out at the lake and wondered if I was beginning to truly lose it in earnest this time. My mind was in turmoil — on one hand it seemed like such an egotistical thing to do, and yet I was learning that the world we see with our eyes is not the true reality; that the grace of God's love is within each of us in powerful ways. The Course promised practical results and I could think of no more practical assistance than to have direct guidance in my daily life.

I stared at the blank piece of paper and picked up the pen in my right hand. What now, I thought. Nothingness of mind is necessary, as in meditation, isn't it? I wondered. Before I could completely empty my mind of these thoughts, I heard a voice within my head which said: "Hosanna. The gift of God is yours. You shall have peace, and love and joy everlasting."

Whatever had occurred, there didn't seem to be any prerequisites. Just willingness. I wrote it down in my large and round handwriting, quickly filling the small page. My mind and heart were racing with connections.

The Bible refers to the "still small voice." The Course promises that "the Holy Spirit is in you in a very literal sense...it is possible even in this world to hear only that voice and no other...it takes effort and great willingness to learn...[for] the Voice for God is always quiet because it speaks of peace." Jesus asks us in the Course to restate the familiar Bible phrase, "my yoke is easy and my burden light" in this way: "Let us join together for My message is light." As I meditated on these things, I sat back in my chair, feeling light hearted and joyful.

One message that came to me after several months of messaging was signed "Franklin." This puzzled me as all of the prior messages had been nameless, and I had the sense that the voice had no gender. Each message had simply closed by hearing an "amen."

It seemed that Franklin was a guide, and clearly wished to identify himself as so. I wondered: could the Holy Spirit be not just a general voice for God, but practical guidance in identity as well? Could we have this personal a relationship with the Holy Spirit? Does this explain the fuzzy thinking I'd always had regarding the meaning of that term? My traditional upbringing was beginning to clash with new ways of looking at the world. Interesting, thought provoking, and certainly unsettling!

Chapter 12

OPEN SPACE

 Our practicing today becomes our gift of thankfulness for release from blindness...Open the curtain in your practicing by merely letting go all things you think you want. Your trifling treasures put away and leave a clean and open space within your mind...
                                        A Course in Miracles

In the spring of 1988, I attended a one-day seminar in Duluth, Minnesota with a close friend. The seminar was on laughter as a healing medicine. It was being given by Annette Goodheart, also known as the laugh lady of Santa Barbara. She was funny and she was smart. As she talked, I began to dwell on a number of things we had in common. We wore our hair similarly and appeared to have similar taste in clothing; she lived on a boat as had I; we led seminars; surely I celebrated her love of laughter; and her stuffed bear, a large, brown cuddly character that she passed around the room to share hugs with, was named Charley. During break, I approached her.

She asked, "And what is it you do exactly?" For some reason, instead of saying that I was an organizational consultant, I answered, "I'm in the business of transforming human hearts." She immediately replied, "Then you must call my secretary and get the phone number and address of Harrison Owen in Maryland. He works with issues of transformation. You'll enjoy him."

I wrote to Harrison the following week. He immediately sent information regarding a conference on organizational transformation scheduled for three weeks hence. This approach and process sounded intriguing and unusual. It was described as a conference without an agenda called Open Space. Participants would be both teachers and students together and would co-create an agenda around their passions and personal quests. I knew I must attend.

It was in that very open space in San Diego, that I found my organizational soul mates, people who see the human spirit and the spiritual path as foundations for the future of the world of work. In this unique gathering of people, I felt I could be exactly who I am, and create a purpose in my work that centers around Spirit. For four and a half days I felt connected to a community that was contemplative, supportive, inclusive, decidedly filled with spirit of its own, and who believed in the worth of High Play. Harrison describes this as "allowing the difficulties of the moment to open to new possibilities, joyfully creating new forms appropriate to an emerging world." I wished fervently that the world of the organization could learn to do this in order to create a living and growing space for all its workers.

My present consulting practice was born that week, exactly nine months after putting a desk in an empty office back home in Bayfield, Wisconsin. Brander and Associates now had some playmates.

I also was turning 50 that month. A woman at the conference heard of this and sought out an unusual shell on the beach. Before she gave it to me, she asked in closing circle on the final morning that the shell be passed through each of the hands in the circle that all present might give it their energy and blessings. This shell still sits on my desk as a reminder of the strength that came to me during my passage into my 50th year.

I have joined in this annual gathering for over eight years now, and can see myself in attendance well into the future. All with thanks to the Laugh Lady of Santa Barbara.

Chapter 13

VAN GO

 ...your Redeemer would have you look upon your brother as yourself...You cannot see the Holy Spirit but you can see your brothers truly. And the light in them will show you all that you need to see.

A Course in Miracles

When I would see Marian Goodlet while doing errands in Bayfield, I would frequently ask about her son, Dick, a quadriplegic from a young age as a result of a diving accident. I had heard that he was back in Bayfield. Although I didn't know him personally, I was well aware of the lack of comprehensive services in the area due to my background of working with people with disabilities. Occasionally I would ask if there was anything I could do to assist her son but nothing seemed apparent.

After one of these encounters, the inner voice spoke of him one day, and I wrote the words: "Help him to walk." I was stunned and laid my pen down immediately. I asked again if I had heard correctly. The answer was clearly "Yes." I was baffled by the meaning of this cryptic message and felt distinct discomfort at the suggestion that such a miracle might occur through something I would do. I chose to ignore it. But I found myself thinking of it, chewing on the possibilities floating around in my mind — all of which struck me as crazy. There seemed to be no way that I could approach it without feeling fearful.

A few days following this I saw Marian again and asked once more if there was anything I could do for Dick. This time she said "Well, he really needs a specially equipped van." Our mutual friend Mary had offered to help financially she said, but "We need to raise some funds too, and we just don't seem to be able to get it going." My mind flew back to the message. Surely this is what was meant! Marian herself had just become a messenger and teacher for me.

I went directly to Dick's apartment and introduced myself. We hit it off immediately and had a grand time talking about the van and other topics. It was also the start of a friendship, an added bonus.

" Count me in," I said to Dick. "I'll chair the efforts and we'll do it." What I didn't know was the power of the Universe when one willingly accepts a role It requests. I called Mary and told her what I had agreed to do, and asked her point blank,

"How much are you good for?" She replied without hesitation, "$2500.00." It was a very solid start.

Next I called Wally Motors in Ashland and described to the owner what we were up to. First he described a used vehicle that cost $16,000. I suggested we lower that amount by a few thousand dollars.

He thought a moment and then said " Well, there is this red van out back that has only 60,000 miles on it, but it has no rear seats....but that's perfect isn't it?"

"How much?" I asked. "$2350." Tom added that he had originally sold and continued to service the van and it was in excellent shape.

"Sold," I said, sight unseen. When I went to Dick's and described in detail the van we had found, his grin said it all.

Within a month the van was being outfitted with a lift, free of charge, by the State of Wisconsin. The family held a fish boil and auction in the waterfront pavilion. The proceeds more than covered the few remaining van alterations. And Dick got his legs.

What a practical means of drawing attention to real concerns these messages were becoming! Each day as I sat in silence in my private space, either in front of my computer or with pad and pen in hand, I opened to a Source of Love that

truly wanted me to receive support for my journey, to see the work to be done, to learn the meaning of service and to see the peace that comes in
those moments when I released any fear that I
might feel.

This voice for God was teaching me that we
are Children of God, that love is our inheritance
and that if our minds can heal into the potential of
unlimited possibilities, that we will discover that
we and all our brethren are the treasure as well as
the pilgrims on this treasure hunt we call life.

Chapter 14

YES I CAN SIR

 God enfolds you in the arms of love. The caress of angel wings is soft. You feel the wonderment of it all. Love enters into your being and warms you from within. Do not flee from your source. We are always here and ready to assist. Be healed in that knowledge.
Message, October 20, 1988

The Shadow side within us asserts itself despite the illumination that is occurring in our lives at any given time. Perhaps that very enlightenment bespeaks of valleys, ravines, bridges (old and new), steep tides, dense flora, distant — and deep — vistas that must be traversed along with these peaks. And Shadow can rise out of the distant past and lay claim over us when we least expect it.

I sat down at my desk in the second floor office I had come to hold dear. The decor of orange shag carpet, orange walls, along with a navy blue hand-me-down couch and an old floppy ceramic lamp (a housewarming joke), felt as dear to me as a Velveteen Rabbit. As I looked out of the window towards the lake, I felt a burst of discomfort in the center of my abdomen. I sucked in my breath. What could be going on?

Picking up a pen and holding it firmly in my right hand, I touched the left side of the legal pad, first line. I dated it October 20, 1988, then moved the point of the pen to the fourth line and waited. Eventually I wrote, "Here I am, Spirit...." and waited again. I mentally asked for help and assurance regarding this pain. It was getting worse. The still small voice began forming words in my head in earnest and as they came, I wrote what I heard: "God enfolds you in the arms of love..."

By the spring of 1988 I had begun to notice digestive problems. The doctor checked my gall-bladder, the customary test on a middle-aged, pudgy female, and reported test results were negative.

By late fall I was in pain and was well aware that the situation was serious. Fortunately I had also been studying Bernie Siegel's writings, practicing Siegel's visualization techniques and, continuing to try to apply the principles of the Course on a daily basis. Illness at this juncture of my life just didn't make any sense, and I was determined to live by my strengthening convictions .

In December, a complete physical by another doctor, including expensive tests, revealed nothing. I called him just before Christmas and said I had plans to visit my son Scott in Montana, but would stay home if there were more tests that we could do. He said "Go, have a good time. You're fine."

In Montana, surrounded by loving family, and having a wonderful time, I knew I was certainly sick. Two bottles of antacid disappeared in a few days time and left no lasting relief.

It was friends Ruth and Jim that came to my rescue. They had come for dinner following my return and, as the four of us sat talking over coffee after dinner, I shared my concern. Ruth said, "You need to go to Marshfield Clinic. It's right up there with Mayo clinic; it's the fifth largest clinic in the nation, and less than four hours south of here. I'll call our friend George who is a doctor there, and he'll get you in."

George in turn referred me to Dr. Bob Phillips. Exactly two weeks later I sat in the doctor's office at the Marshfield Clinic and answered questions for over an hour. The tests were performed the next week and when Dr. Nunez, informally known as "Poncho," did the colonoscopy, he found the cancer. It was at least a stage three tumor and had grown outside the colon wall. Were it a stage four tumor, the cancer would be obviously metastasized and little could be done. I needed surgery immediately.

Those who have been told "You have a cancerous tumor" know full well the impact of listening to these words. I felt as if in shock. The office staff was most supportive. They assisted me in scheduling the operation but when I heard it would not take place for over three weeks, I protested.

"No way, I need surgery now, not three weeks from now. I need to feel better now, not ten weeks from now." The surgical nurse looked at me for a few seconds in silence. Then she called the scheduling department back and said, "We have this spiffy lady here who's in a hurry. We need to schedule next week." I thanked her with my tears.

It was Bob who put it into perspective as we drove home in silence. He said, "Diane, we've just completed step one of this process. You finally know what's wrong and you're scheduled for surgery next Wednesday. We really needed to know this. Step two is next and it's the surgery and recuperation. There's not much sense in worrying about step three because the verdict may be positive and you may not need follow-up treatment. So let's just concentrate on step two and get you well." It was sound advice.

I needed love and prayer more than anything else, so I spent the weekend calling everyone in the country I could think of that could offer support. I saw a fly on the wall on Saturday night in our living room and thought of Siegel's advice to literally see the cancer disappear through whatever visioning process worked. So I danced, I whirled and I sang with the music, pretending that the fly was the cancer. I danced and I sang and the fly disappeared. I said goodbye to it, clearly, firmly and with great conviction.

I used the word "cancer" frequently during the weekend, despite admiring the school of thought that says "do not own the disease by naming it." I felt this was the only way I could conquer the fear that this word carries. So I used it over and over and, when people would say the usual "How are you?" I would reply, "Not so good. I've got cancer!"

On January 23, 1989 I packed my bag. Feeling it crucial to have all my special books and tapes with me in the hospital, I threw in Siegel and Norman Cousins. They teach that humor is one of the essential components of this adventure, so I packed my moose slippers and my banana-nose glasses as well.

I had also apprised the surgeon of my strong spiritual foundation and my belief in miracles. I asked him to honor that by not being negative in any way despite what he might find when he operated. It was important as well that I be called Diane, not Mrs. Brander, since I was in a whole new ball game here and needed that personal recognition. (I added that I never go by Mrs. anyway.)

He said he wasn't sure he could do that. He didn't say why. I assumed it was because of his adherence to mainstream, impersonal, medical tradition. Whatever the explanation, he was right. He couldn't call me Diane. So he didn't call me by any name, at least to my face, for nine days.

Following a decidedly unromantic 24 hours in a motel with Bob and a colonic preparation, I arrived at the hospital on Tuesday with my squeaky clean colon. The first words the nurse spoke were, "Hi. It's time for your enema."

Well, no, I said frankly. First I would be setting up my room and then I would be visiting the chapel. Then she could ply her trade. This was undoubtedly the first of many incidents that got me dubbed a difficult patient. In much of medicine, and particularly in hospital settings, the patient is often treated like an impersonal object without any role to play in the process. But what's worse is that patients accept it.

My conversation with this nurse took a delightful turn however. She came to my bedside the first night and said, "You strike me as someone who would appreciate a single room. It's really crowded in here with your roommate in her eighth week of stay, and a single just became available. What do you say?" I jumped at the chance.

Bob was supportive and loving despite his fear of the outcome. The night before surgery we sat in the waiting room of the surgery floor holding hands and saying little. Finally Bob murmured, "Let's change the channel."

I nodded. Then I decided it was time for him to know of the inner guidance, the messages of hope and love that I had been receiving throughout my illness. We went to the room where I read three messages aloud to him. When I finished I added, "This voice is the Voice for God. Believe in It, Bob, for It is every bit as real to me as are you. It seems a single voice yet a union of spirit. Perhaps this is the meaning of Brander and Associates."

As I shared this with him, he was crying. I confided that I had been assured continuously for eight months by this gentle inner voice that healing and wholeness were mine if I would remain calm and release any fear. There was no fear within me as I sat with him that night. I prayed the same would be true for him.

The surgeon performed skillfully. I received a great outpouring of love from family and many friends. Friends of many years, Lloyd and Pat, drove seven hours to visit with me, and cousin

Tara and her husband Jerry were there to add to family. I let all of these healing sources wash over and through me, bringing their own unique energies to my healing body.

On Day Three I calmly awaited the lab reports. Despite the fact that I "should" have been filled with cancer, the report investigating cancerous residue was negative. They inspected over 50 lymph nodes surrounding the locale and there wasn't a trace. Can I say for certain that this was a miracle? No. But it was good enough for me. Evidently it was good enough for my favorite resident and a couple of nurses also, for I got hugs from them upon hearing the news.

Ironically, it wasn't good enough for my surgeon who came into the room the day after the report. "Hi, Frank," I said, as he walked in. I asked him if he had heard the news.

"What news?" He asked.

"The good news on the lab report!" I replied.

He said grimly, "Yes, I saw the report...but I don't want to give you too much hope."

"Perhaps," I replied tensely "I need to remind you of our initial conversation. If you insist on such negativity, you best leave."

He must have decided that I was acting "menopausal" because the next thing I knew a female oncologist showed up in my room. She sat rigidly in front of me attempting to explain my chances of survival by using statistics.

"There is a 20 percent chance that this cancer will recur," she stated convincingly.

"Wonderful," I replied smiling broadly. "That means the odds are eighty percent that I will never experience it again. That leaves just twenty percent remaining for God and me. We can do it!" She didn't return my smile.

I walked the corridors each day wearing my moose slippers. If each patient on the floor had been given different animal slippers, we could have had a whole zoo parading around the corridors. Just think what that would do for morale and healing, not to mention that we could get to know one another and laugh a little together. "Hey, here comes Ms. Piggie and Mr. Skunk. How're ya doin?"

I saved the banana-nose glasses for my last day, for by then I knew that a parade of residents would troop into the room at about six a.m. That morning I put on the glasses, pulled the covers up under my chin and pretended I was asleep. The first person through the door was a complete stranger to me who, later I found out, was the head resident. Although he was obviously baffled by this 50-year-old female who was supposed to be sick, the other residents were doubled-up with stifled laughter behind him. He managed to stammer a greeting but didn't stay long. Even Mr. Surgeon, who heard the story through the grapevine, wore a smile when he came by to release me.

I loved the irreverence. So did many others who heard the story as it spread through the hospital. Perhaps the hospital staff yearned for change in their sterile environment as much as did I. We all deserve to let our creativity out, to celebrate our uniqueness, to work and heal in a loving, supportive environment, and to have a laugh in the midst of insanity. It's definitely difficult in a traditional hospital setting.

One issue I had to come to terms with in all of this was trying to understand why I had gotten so ill while on such a powerful path in my life. The answer came just before I left the hospital.

Poncho stopped by to say goodbye and, without my asking, said, "You know this cancer started about five or six years prior to this, don't you?" I had not known that. But when I thought more about it, I realized that this coincided with a most difficult time in my life, the death of my mother. The lesson I apparently needed to learn revolves around what happens when we refuse to let go of guilt, blame and sorrow. I silently vowed to review all aspects of my life with her. I was apparently being asked to release and let go. This was a tall order.

I sighed deeply and snuggled down in the bed, pulling the covers up to my chin. This time no banana nose and no laughter.

In seven weeks I was back on the road sporting my semi-colon and feeling better than ever. I tape-recorded my feelings as I was driving down highway 35 towards Minneapolis that spring:

"Today is the first day...ha!...of the rest of my life. Indeed! The first day since surgery seven weeks ago. And I cannot describe the feelings I am experiencing. I've been feeling this all day. It's a sense of energy, a sense of purpose. Not that I have any real notion of what the purpose might be. I'm joyful. I'm very much alive and filled with gratitude. A great deal of that gratitude is for the experience I have just been through. I have had total courage, strength and peace of mind since I was told I had cancer. I have never tested my faith like this before. It is powerful. It's awesome. I now know that the teachings I have been studying for the past two-and-a-half years in the Course are manifesting themselves in my life on a daily basis. Somehow this all goes back to the storm in 1984, the beginning of a series of events that have led us to now. I am happy as hell, and exceedingly joy-filled. I'm feeling that we, the family, the Associates are on the brink of something very, very big."

Chapter 15

INKLINGS, 1990

 By [the] refusal to attempt to teach yourself what you do not know, the Guide Whom God has given you will speak to you. He will take his rightful place in your awareness the instant you abandon it, and offer it to Him.
A Course in Miracles

Our life became very full. Bob's world expanded and demanded talents of him that amazed even him. My business took me into several states and I began working with two additional universities. Contacts were primarily by word of mouth, for I felt it important to try to apply faith in all aspects of life. This became scary when there were weeks of blanks on my calendar. But somehow they always seemed to fill with the right amount of work.

The house was transforming, room by room, into a truly beautiful home. New friends, Greg and Betty, moved into the house across the street. With their energy, concern for others and generous good humor we began to create a true community in our neighborhood. Prosperity and abundance manifested in many ways in our lives in just three short years of our return to Bayfield.

A niggling little idea began taking form. Sometimes it was more like a feeling. Often it came as a daydream. Occasionally it came as an actual message from an inner voice:

"Believe in the miracle that is about to unfold. It becomes a part of your story — to be told over and over to those who wait. Can you feel the excitement? Relish it. Joy is ever present." (August 20, 1990)

"The nonprofit is to be started just as Brander and Associates was...on faith, and without all of the answers. Robert is part of the plan. He will understand. Space will be provided as you are told and it will be a center for teaching, healing and hope...it will be removed from the everyday world." (December 14, 1990)

"You are giving birth...The target is fall of 1991." (April 29, 1991)

Once it came in the form of a map I was to draw of the United States, then Wisconsin, then Bayfield County. I was then asked to place a dot west of Washburn in Bayfield County.

Another time I drew a picture with my markers while thinking of this persistent idea. The drawing that emerged was of a large, open, green space with trees and landscape which looked out over a lake.

The idea seemed to be that I was to create a center. It seemed to be a space for issues of personal and social transformation, a loving space for healing and growth, for co-creation and celebration.

I was concerned. Who was I to think I could take on such a challenge? How could I ever explain to Bob that there was more beyond this beautiful Bayfield existence we now enjoyed?

The only friend I dared even mention this to was Brenda Dettmann, a dear friend of many years. We had met Brenda and Don at a Marriage Encounter in Duluth in the late 70's. Brenda is a deeply spiritual human being. When I told her about my vision, she didn't laugh. She encouraged me and listened closely to my feelings about it. She related a daydream she had had many years earlier where she saw herself working in a retreat center.

So we giggled and dreamed together. What we were doing without knowing it was learning to give form and substance to a little understood request from a higher realm of existence.

In February of 1991, Bob and I were driving to Duluth to catch a plane to the Bahamas for a well deserved vacation with the Fun Hogs. This group was comprised of some of our favorite folks from the Bayfield and Washburn area who basically liked to kick back and enjoy life. Bob and I had left a day early because I was giving a presentation in Duluth that day.

Public Radio was airing the Jean Feraca show. She announced that her guest for the next day would be Melanie Keveles, co-author of *Fired for Success.*

"I really have to meet Melanie," I observed out loud. "She's been mentioned to me frequently lately, and sounds very much like my kind of person."

He dropped me off at the meeting site and, as I walked in the door a woman darted across the entry and said, "Hi. I'm Melanie Keveles..." By now I am not surprised at much of anything, but I truly love the timing of this one.

Mel is also a student of *A Course in Miracles*, a writer and, as she laughingly describes herself a "cross-pollinating arousal agent." She is primarily a career counselor, but all the other titles are true as well.

Over a six-hour dinner we compared dreams, and Mel became a second source of inspiration for me. Memories of Brenda and Mel's love and support are precious. Both women became important sources of support for the vision.

A significant event with Bob and me occurred in the spring of 1991. I was increasingly certain that the center was calling me. Although I didn't know what this meant, I knew that I had to go where this was leading me.

I frequently sat in my office, thinking of the powerful role Bob had played in my life since we met in 1972. I remembered with sharp clarity — and pain — the early years when there were continuous struggles in our lives. Our world was filled with vast complexities, and I often wondered how we lasted through the tumult and the confusion. There were the usual issues of a new relationship between two strong people. There were our pasts and old relationships, a blended family and all its dramatic dynamics, and our moves from community to community. Our jobs were often difficult, and we both fell into outbursts of immaturity. Bob occasionally became violent. And I felt a separation from God at that time, a time when we desperately needed support and solace.

The years in the Virgin Islands and on the boat had matured us. Bob captained our vessel with incomparable strength and devotion and I felt great admiration for him and for us. We were far from perfect but we had a foundation that was built out of shared struggle. We didn't feel like victims any more. We were survivors, and I believed that our relationship was beginning to evidence more of the flavor of a truly committed partnership.

But, in honesty, I had felt cheated at times during these years. And that was no longer acceptable to me. I had, on several occasions during the marriage chosen to follow his lead rather than my own inner lead. And while I believe that it usually turned out for the best, I was very certain that this time there must be no wavering on my part. I was coming to this place of purpose in my life with total commitment, wherever it would take me. What would Bob choose?

Bob and I also took divergent religious views. We didn't see eye to eye on *A Course in Miracles* nor did we necessarily agree on Christianity in general. Bob was critical of organized religion. We enjoyed debating about these things but, of course, never changed one another's mind. So how would he react to something based entirely on a voice and a vision?

Another concern was our home. The sweat of Bob's brow was in every aspect of this second house on the ravine. How could he ever leave it? Especially for some cockamamie idea that I swore Spirit had dreamed up? What was I going to do?

Several days later I knew. I was certain that I was going to have to stand tall, to speak my truth and trust in my guidance, no matter what. I realized I was at a crossroads and would walk on through and out the other side. I could wait for no one.

I went up to Bob in the kitchen on a cloudy afternoon and asked him to sit at the table. I drew a diagram on a piece of paper and tried to picture for him what happens when we reach a transformative stage in our lives. I borrowed from Harrison Owen's concepts of change, and sketched the free fall into open space and eventually the point of being down at the bottom, in the dumps.

"This is where we go through lots of grief for the old and the reimagination of the new," I said. I pointed to the steep climb up the other side to a new way of being and said to Bob, "I'm headed up this hill and I'm going over the top. That's where true learning takes place. I need to tell you my fears."

I shared with my husband and partner the agonizing hours in my office and then I said, "I'm going to go on, with or without you. Something is driving me and I feel you might be uncomfortable with what is coming. So what we are and what we have been may be over."

He looked at me with pain in his eyes and said, "Are you saying that everything that's been wrong in this relationship is my fault?"

"Of course not." I said. "There is no right or

wrong, fault or blame. It isn't even about us. It's about total commitment on my part to go where this leads me. And I'm going to go, with or without you."

Then I'm going with you," he said simply.

I jumped up and threw my arms about him. He was willing! My relief was enormous.

I had just received the greatest gift he could give to me — his faith in my path. We had, for some indefinite period of time, switched places at the tiller. Despite his scientific training and experience, he was willing to risk ridicule and follow an uncertain course. And neither of us knew where it would lead.

Chapter 16

THE VISION

 Put your complete faith and trust in Me, and know that I will never fail or forsake you. Nothing you undertake is impossible, for you can do all things with Me. Live by faith. I want you to see good come out of every situation no matter how seemingly strange the situation may appear to be... Are you willing to step out in complete faith and do the seemingly impossible, not out of bravado, but because you know without a shadow of a doubt where it comes from?

Eileen Caddy

The summer of 1991, Melanie and I decided to go to the annual Open Space Conference together. We had messaged prior to going to the airport and were promised delights upon arrival. Mel had listened to her inner voice and while she spoke, I wrote what she shared. In a stream of consciousness, she related that we would sup in splendor and see castles in the mountains and this would be our greeting once in Colorado.

Unfortunately we chose to panic over a confused plane schedule in Duluth. We were already on board and excitedly chattering about the trip

when it was announced that there was a malfunc-
tion on the plane. We were all asked to exit and
return to the main ticket counter for rescheduling.
There was little leeway to our schedule and we
wondered nervously what to do. The best choice
seemed to be to reschedule our Minneapolis flight
for five hours later in the day.

Just as we were handed new tickets, the
announcement came over the loudspeaker:
"Please reboard. The plane will be departing in
ten minutes."

On the way to Minneapolis it was clear that
we would have approximately fifteen minutes to
make the next plane. So we worked out a game
plan where Mel would run to the next gate and tell
them of our arrival on the originally scheduled flight
and I would schlep the luggage on a cart to that
gate as soon as possible.

I made it to the gate with what I thought was
one minute to spare only to see Mel turn to me
forlornly and say, "They won't let us on because
we don't have tickets for this flight any more." No
amount of begging the gate official changed
things.

We laid over in Minneapolis for five hours and
arrived at midnight in Denver to a La Quinta motel
and dinner at Denny's. Not at all what we had envisioned.

But no fault of the guidance Mel had received, we decided. While flying to Denver we processed the *choice* we had made to panic (distinct from panicking) and shared concern that we had stepped on our faith by fearing the worst. "Kaufman says happiness is a choice," said Mel. "And so is anger, fear, control and panic."

"If we had simply trusted in the plane connections" I added, "we would have enjoyed an extra day in the mountains." Apparently, we concluded, we needed further confidence in our guidance and well-being in order for faith to tide us through daily surprises. So we tried to find castles in the clouds as we flew, and laughed uproariously when one would appear.

The week was spectacular. We were high in the Rockies at a resort near Winter Park. The condos were inviting and spacious and the mountain air invigorating. The community that gathered annually in Open Space was filled with old friends as well as many new attendees.

It was in our luxurious condo that the visioning experience occurred. My friend Charley Tack was facilitating the afternoon. When I said I was coming, he replied, "Oh, this is much too basic for you. Don't bother." I reluctantly agreed and decided to go for a walk. But I ended up at the visioning anyway.

What got me there was the need for a bath-room. While in the condo my curiosity was peaked so I snuck into an ample space behind one of the living room couches. The room was full of partici-pants, and Charley had already started introduc-ing the session.

He was explaining that we could ask the uni-verse a question, any question, and the vision quest would attempt to answer it. I couldn't resist. I decided to ask about the center. Having no idea what to ask for specifically, and feeling rushed to decide, I formulated the simple question: What does it look like?

Charlie asked us to relax and go within, to find a safe physical space in our mind's eye and go there. I chose my office space in our house in Bayfield, which was now located downstairs in the back of the house in a very private and quiet room. We were asked to invite in a guide to assist us in our quest. I first asked our dog Charley Noble to come in. Then I looked up to see a beautiful, wispy woman figure appear; she softly said her name was Spirit Woman. She settled across the room from me.

Charley Tack now asked us to picture a con-ference room, one that was safe and beautiful for us, and to configure a table or a circle on the floor — what ever felt good. I decided to stay in the office space and to be seated on the floor. I asked Spirit Woman to be seated across from me and she gracefully floated into place. Charley Noble was at my feet.

We were encouraged to invite in one or two other guides. An opportunity was presenting itself. I had never "met" Franklin in any form. I asked for him.

He came into the room dressed in western style jeans, boots, and a shirt, but wearing a startlingly beautiful Eagle mask. He sat on my right. Charley Noble moved over next to him.

Our leader suggested we should invite in any additional guidance we would find helpful. I thought about this and decided that Jesus would be about as helpful a guide as I could imagine. But I was concerned that his presence might dazzle me with light. So I asked that He come just as He walked the earth, clothed in simple garb and very human.

Jesus came silently into the room, smiled, touched my shoulder, and sat on my left side. His presence was filled with peace and I was totally comfortable.

We were now being instructed to follow the lead of our guides and allow whatever was going to happen to take place. I smiled at my circle of companions, shrugged my shoulders and awaited instructions.

We were immediately flying out of the conference room up into the ether. We were all joined
arm in arm, almost like a scene out of the Wizard
of Oz. Down below us were northern white and
red pine and forest, green and lush.

Suddenly there was an opening in the forest
below and we descended into a small grove of
trees and touched our feet upon the earth. Charley Noble bounded ahead down a path that appeared at the edge of this space.

As the guides started down the path I was told
to follow them. The path was winding and well
worn. The earth was gentle under our feet and the
forest was dense.

The guides then stood aside, I walked forward
and Jesus took my hand. We both ducked as He
led me under some apple trees, for the branches
were low to the ground and unpruned. He stopped
as we reached an open space, and motioned me
on ahead.

I was standing at the bottom of a large, open,
gently sloping hill. There were trees all around the
rim of the hill. On the right side of the hill, at the
top, was a beautiful brown building. It looked like
a lodge. The view was very natural and the land
appeared filled with spirit. The feeling within me
was one of immense peace and I was transfixed. I
heard not a sound.

I had no notion of how long I stood there, but too soon I heard Charley's voice suggesting that we prepare to return to our conference room with our guides. I turned and we were immediately flying back towards Bayfield and the office. We settled into our spaces by descending through the roof of the house as if this were an everyday occurrence. I wanted to thank my guides, and gift them each with love and gratitude for their help. We parted after honoring each other, one at a time. Jesus hugged me and I wept. With the gentle brush of his hand, he wiped away my tears before he disappeared.

Charley Tack's voice called us back to the condo in Winter Park. I didn't want to go. But soon I was fully alert and stretching my cramped body, still scrunched behind the couch. I was not the same as when I left. Something had shifted within. I realized I was crying again but I was exhilarated as well. I knew I had seen the center that called to me.

The people in the room shared for several more minutes while I lay there and listened, knowing I could not share what I had experienced without choking up. So I waited until all but Charley, my roommates and Toby, a friend, had left and then popped up from behind the couch. "You guys will never believe what I just experienced!" I grinned. "Thank God for bathrooms!"

Chapter 17

NEW HORIZONS

 The world is fair because the Holy Spirit has brought injustice to the light within, and there has all injustice been resolved and replaced with justice and with love.

A Course in Miracles

Mel, Joanne, Charley, Toby and I were relaxing in the living room. We had all been sharing excitedly in the visioning of the afternoon and I had just finished telling my story and was feeling emotionally drained by the retelling. My companions were sharing in the excitement. The phone interrupted our conversation. It was Bob calling.

Horizon, our amazon of the storm, had been sold on a contract basis to Joel in 1985. We had sailed south to Florida while Joel continued to anchor Horizon in the Chesapeake. For three years Joel had been faithful in his payments, or had sent what he could. But the fourth year payments began to get more scarce and we were beginning to get concerned. He owed a great deal on his contract and we counted on that monthly check. So we had decided to pay him a visit that fall.

Bob and I had gone to the Chesapeake while visiting family in Delaware. The boat was in Solomons Island but Joel was not. Through some sleuthing, we discovered he was staying with his brother in Alexandria, Virginia, so we called him there. He agreed to meet with us at his brother's house the next day. But when we arrived we were told Joel had left for a job interview and would not be available. The disappointment gave way to fear and frustration. What were we to do if he started to run? Repossessing a boat hundreds of miles from our home was no small feat.

We decided to go back to the restaurant where we had lunched prior to the appointment. We had time to kill and wanted to discuss our next step.

As we pulled up to the restaurant, there was Joel standing on the steps. His brother was pulling into the opposite drive to pick him up. They spotted us and Joel disappeared inside as his brother sped off. It felt like we were actors in some kind of zany movie. We rushed inside but no Joel.

Now we were really perplexed. We debated between calling for help and trying to relocate him. As we sat there, Joel appeared and feigned great surprise at seeing us in the restaurant.

"Let's not pretend any further, Joel," I said. He apologized and we went ahead with our meeting. All the while he insisted that he fully intended to pay us.

The money came twice more. Then we were informed by colleagues in the Chesapeake that Horizon had left the Solomon's Island area and was headed south on the Inland Waterway. It was the last time we received a check. It was the last time we saw Horizon or heard from Joel. We managed to locate him at his brother's house by telephone soon after the boat disappeared. He basically said the boat was hidden.

"You will never find her," he asserted. Joel concluded by announcing that he was through paying us and there wasn't a thing we could do about it.

We had indeed felt hog tied. After a detective turned up nothing, I asked my associates for guidance and was told to let it go, that justice would be served in another way. So the only other step we took was to send out a few fliers to places along the Inland Waterway. We offered a picture of Horizon and a small reward if she was found. It had now been months since we had done that and I no longer was dwelling on it.

Bob's voice affirmed a change. "We've had a call. We've located Horizon," he said. "She's hidden in a little boat yard near Beaufort, North Carolina. We need to get there immediately and take legal possession." We left for North Carolina the day I returned from Colorado.

Thus it was that Horizon came back to us once again. But we had sold Sopris long ago; the vision of the sailing life was complete, at least for now. We simply put Horizon up for auction and she was sold for a small sum, enough to pay all the expenses of locating and repossessing her. In the worldly view of such matters we had lost big time, but in the larger picture, I believe everyone received something. We learned that it wasn't necessary to bear malice towards Joel. He, of course, had possession of Horizon for several years. The new owner got a deal financially. And she had saved our lives. What else mattered? When I look back on this I not only see that one piece of the odyssey had completed itself in its own unique way, but I marvel at the timing. Another path had just opened itself to us.

Chapter 18

NEW REALITY

 Expect a miracle. Expect miracle upon miracle to come about, and do not limit in any way. The more open you are, the better, for there is nothing in the way to stop the flow of My laws, for miracles are simply My laws in action.

Eileen Caddy

One month after the vision in Colorado I was standing in the Bayfield Post Office licking stamps and conversing with our realtor, Donna. As we talked the voice suggested I speak up concerning the center. I mentally argued with this, but to no avail, for my mouth said, "Donna, I'm looking for property for a retreat center. Do you know of any-thing?"

She promptly replied, "Well, this 86 acre farm just came on the market. I hear it's beautiful, with lots of buildings, a view of Lake Superior, a pond, woods. I haven't seen it yet myself. Let's drive out on Saturday. It's just 17 miles from here."

Already I was thinking of how I would an-nounce this to Bob, who was at that very moment putting the absolute finishing touches to our home after four and one-half years of renovation.

Saturday morning arrived with pouring rain. At ten o'clock Donna honked her horn and she and I were off to Washburn and the countryside nearby. I had bravely admitted to Bob that I was looking at real estate and he had shot me a look of absolute incredulity. No comment necessary.

As we neared the driveway I prayed that I would be free of any expectations, and asked that I be open to the disappointment that could occur. The writeup on the property had been intriguing. The only thing that threw me was the price.

The mailbox appeared, and we swung north onto a sand and gravel drive that proceeded through the woods about a quarter of a mile. The tree-lined drive felt safe. We might easily be moving back in time, I thought, as we slowly drove along in the rain.

We arrived at an old farmstead and Donna paused briefly. She pointed out a two-story farmhouse to our right. There was a certain attractive character to its simple lines. It was covered in asphalt shingle though, and that connoted a decision to be practical, rather than continually repaint old clapboard that most likely was original with the building. My mind was already re-siding this lovely little house.

A stone ice-house stood to its left, snuggled

into a tiny hillside. This small building was instantly pleasing. I wanted to run up and fling open its doors to see what possibilities lay within. Donna's voice brought me back.

"Across from the house and back in the woods," she said, "you can see the roof of a one-room cabin. I understand that this is used as a guest house now."

She once again caught my attention and we shifted our eyes to the barn, a large one-story building to our left. It had an unusually low roof, with stone walls leaning threateningly inward — and outward. These walls seemed about to collapse on spaces where vibrant life had long ago throbbed. A wood and stone calving pen and chicken coop were attached. These were places of mystery that had once housed animals and sheltered the people who had farmed here. Mossy rocks were everywhere and I felt the spirit of these buildings and this land beginning to draw me in. Stone walls were evident as were the remains of a greenhouse in the underbrush near the barn.

I thought of the vision in Colorado. What I was seeing here was flat, no hill, no view. I nodded with appreciation thinking, close, but no cigar.

Then Donna said, "But the real treasure is up on the hill." She drove on, curved left above the barn and then followed the drive onward to the right which put us on the top of a gently sloping hill. I could not see through the steady rain what lay at the bottom but the hill was part forest, part open.

We were pulling up to a brown lodge. It was encased in stones and the wood structure rose out of a stone foundation like a bermed house rises out of the earth. I stepped out into the rain. My heart was racing. This all fit the vision, but I was looking downhill instead.

I mentally put myself at the bottom of this hillside, and what I saw was a large, open, sloping hill with trees all around the rim. At the top, right-hand side of the hill was this beautiful lodge.

We walked quickly to the door to escape the rain. A stately, silver-haired woman opened the door and welcomed us inside. Her name was Frances Seagraves. We entered into a long narrow porch-like living area with a huge fieldstone fireplace midway down the room. This space also contained a dining area and kitchen. The entire interior was cypress. Frances asked Donna and me to look around at our leisure.

I walked slowly left and passed between two French doors into a formal vaulted living room where I discovered another huge fieldstone fireplace. I was visually overwhelmed. This was the stuff dreams are made of.

My practical self emerged and immediately reminded me that I had forgotten a very important detail of the vision in Colorado. There were apple trees. As I was thinking this I glanced over at the leaded casement windows lining the front of the lodge and looked out into an apple orchard. Any possible objections took a nosedive as the realization swept over me that I was standing on the land of the vision; there was absolutely no doubt.

I was there! There is here! The tears flowed down my cheeks with the enormity of this discovery. I stood there motionless for at least a minute trying to calm my racing heart. Finally I turned and faced the others in the room. There was an enormous smile on my face.

Chapter 19

COMMITMENT

*i thank You God for most this amazing
day:for the leaping greenly spirits of trees
and a blue true dream of sky; and for everything
which is natural which is infinite which is yes*

*(I who have died am alive again today,
and this is the sun's birthday; this is the birth day
of life and of love and wings: and of the gay
great happening illimitably earth)...*

*(now the ears of my ears awake and
now the eyes of my eyes are opened)*
e.e. cummings

It seemed an eternity before I could arrange for Bob to see the land. In fact, it was two weeks. He had been totally thrown by the appearance of an actual piece of land, and was quite reluctant to even take a look. I begged him to come and promised he wouldn't be disappointed.

We set aside a Saturday that was, thanks be to Great Spirit, drenched in sunshine and warmth. As we climbed into the car I started chattering about all of the buildings, the pond and wooded areas. By the time we drove into the drive he had already had a mental tour of the 86 acres.

After slowly walking the land from building to building, we discovered yet another building tucked behind a small hill east of the lodge. It had been the cookhouse, Frances told us. It had been used years earlier to house the summer help who cooked for the visitors in the lodge. An old cook stove still stood beyond the rotting doorway, amidst years of use by the animal kingdom it seemed. Droppings were everywhere, especially those of Porcupine.

"The Potters owned this farm," she said. "Alden Potter was a physician from Massachusetts who had given up his medical practice having become a Christian Scientist. Evidently he felt the two were incompatible." I thrilled at what Frances had just shared with us, knowing that Christian Science healing is based solely on faith in God and reliance on God's truth. This unique religion had helped shore me up during my bout with cancer. My close friend Shirley and her family had given me Mary Baker Eddy's book, *Science and Health*. "How appropriate," I murmured.

Frances continued her story. "Doc Potter sold real estate in Minneapolis, and around 1912, decided to move to Northern Wisconsin and become a farmer. He built this place in its entirety in just two years time, digging the rocks from the earth and putting them to use in the buildings. Of course the land had been clear-cut before the turn of the century and most of the original white and red Pine are gone. I'll show you the stumps. Potter's the one who converted the property to farmland."

The farmstead was home base for Doc Potter, Frances added, and the lodge was built as a three-season home for the rest of his family. It was at that time just two bedrooms, a living room and a long screened porch, but he spared no expense with the elegant cypress interior and stone fireplaces.

Frances and Michael Seagraves had since retired to the lodge for the spring, summer and fall of each year and had installed indoor plumbing and converted a portion of the porch into a kitchen. They had also planted pine and spruce on much of the property, wisely leaving a large, open space with a view of Lake Superior between the lodge and farmhouse. There was an abundance of trees, diverse in their nature, white pine, red pine, Austrian pine, Norway and Colorado spruce, apple trees, pear trees, grape arbors, aspen, maple and others.

A path wound its way into the woods past a pond in the northwest corner of the property. Frances pointed with pride to her reforestation projects and took us to the old dam and well in the woods, at one time a key part of the farm.

"Greta married Doc Potter in 1932," Frances continued. "She's a piece of this place as well. They were married only four years when he died, and after cremation his ashes were scattered on this hilltop. She kept the land 'til the fifties when we bought it for our hidey-hole. Greta was an unusual woman for her day; highly educated, loved adventure and was a Christian Science Reader herself. That's probably how they met."

Frances told us of Greta's poetry which spoke of her love for this land. Back in the lodge, she handed a book to me entitled *Chequamegon View Hilltop* and said, "Here. Read for yourself. It's a signed copy." We were enthralled with Frances' stories and deep connection with this place, and intrigued by Greta and Alden Potter.

Once Bob had walked the land with me, he began to share, ever so slightly in my excitement. He raised serious questions from the beginning about the financial aspects of this project which he secretly saw as financial suicide. But the gift he gave and gave without limits was his absolute faith in my vision. He had committed to going with me and he meant it.

The asking price was far beyond our means. We put it on hold for a week, not knowing what to do. During that week we received a phone call from a friend who now lived in Alaska but had formerly lived near the farm. Kate was not only familiar with the area but knew the precise property we were speaking of.

Kate said, "That's one of my favorite pieces of property anywhere in the area. But the asking price is quite a bit higher than what it was appraised for a couple of years ago. I know because we spoke with the appraiser."

Bingo! Bob and I discussed this piece of news and decided to make an offer. The Seagraves responded with a generously reduced counter offer. We accepted the terms with a provision that we sell the house in Bayfield prior to closing. It was, as the message of April 29, 1991 had predicted, the fall of 1991.

I couldn't contain my excitement. Bob would make light of the farm by teasing me about this mad fixation when we were with others, but when we were alone, he talked often of it. It appeared that the spirit of these grounds had touched him as well by calling to his sense of adventure, his love of challenge and his kinship with the earth.

Chapter 20

BIRTHING

 Eagle medicine is the power of the Great Spirit, the connection to the Divine. It is the ability to live in the realm of Spirit, and yet remain connected and balanced within the realm of Earth. Eagle soars, and is quick to observe expansiveness within the overall pattern of life. From the heights of the clouds, Eagle is close to the heavens where the Great Spirit dwells.

Jamie Sams and David Carson

I was sure that the right buyer for our house would appear immediately. But little happened at all, at least with the house. The messages were becoming much more specific in content and my faith deepened as the falling leaves piled high. One day while thinking about the meaning of the center to be founded on the farm, I recalled my fascination with the Findhorn Foundation in Scotland and pulled out *The Magic of Findhorn* to reread it. This story of a walk of faith had moved me deeply some 16 years before, and I began to feel parallels between the center of light that is Findhorn and the center we hoped to create at the farm.

Perhaps, I mused, we ought to visit Findhorn.

The more I thought about that possibility, the more excited and convinced I became. I wrote to the Findhorn Foundation, obtained flight schedules, worked out a budget, and decided to keep it all as a surprise Christmas present for Bob. The joy I felt made up for the fact that there was little interest in our beautiful house in Bayfield.

An event occurred on October 9th of that year that spoke still more of the mysteries afoot. I had left town to pick up Melanie in Superior, Wisconsin. We were going on a business trip to northern Minnesota. As I pulled onto Highway 2 and started my sixty-mile drive to Mel's, I saw a large object on the highway in the distance. No other cars were in sight in either direction. I approached the object at a fairly fast clip and only slowed when I realized I was driving straight towards a bald eagle. She was looking directly at me, not budging an inch.

I came to a complete stop and we locked eyes. There was no carrion on the highway to explain her insistent presence there. I stared as if in a trance for about ten seconds. She then rose up off the ground and circled above the car, finally flying ahead of me no more than twenty feet above the highway. I followed slowly behind her, mesmerized. She circled again, flew back over the car and swooped up into the sky. I stopped, got out of the car and looked up. She was gone.

That night while Mel and I were in our hotel room, the phone rang. It was my son Scott, calling to tell me that my first grandchild, Jarrett McKenzie, had been born that day. Jarrett had started his journey into the world at exactly the time I had encountered Eagle. "The baby and Annie are doing fine," Scott said.

Well, I guess so! According to the Medicine Way taught by many Native Americans, Eagle embodies Spirit and is sacred to many who follow the Native way. This visitation was an honor to me and I was grateful to be touched in such a powerful manner. It was definitely a Bald Eagle Day.

Despite the occasional doubts concerning the lack of interest in the house (it wasn't happening my way after all) the excitement of a trip to Findhorn occupied my mind. I carefully concocted a collection of clues that I wrapped in a bright shiny green box with red bow to put under the tree for Bob. Jean, his mother, daughter Catherine and son-in-law David, would be with us for Christmas, which made it even more exciting. Jean is not only the dearest mother-in-law possible but also has been a strong supporter of my dream for a center. I had told her of Bob's gift, and she had smiled her approval.

Bob opened the box slowly and read each clue, one at a time. He was initially confused by them, then amazed at what they spelled out, and finally embarrassed by such a lavish gift. I smiled broadly and said, "You'll get used to it." Catherine and David, both veteran European travelers, soon had his attention with lots of helpful tips for the journey.

From Christmas until late February we busily planned our two weeks in Scotland. We each needed to write our own reasons for wishing to attend Experience Week at Findhorn Foundation. I wrote mine swiftly. Only at the last minute did Bob leave his statement on my desk.

He had eloquently expressed his commitment to be a caretaker of the living spirit of Lake Superior, a mission he had evolved through a lifetime connection with this extraordinary element of nature. His father had been a lighthouse keeper on Lake Superior and in the St Mary's River, and Bob's upbringing was the greenhouse in which grew seeds planted from birth. The seeds were truly beginning to blossom as he described in his application his dedication and resolve, his deep passion for the lake.

His statement was referred to with obvious admiration in our acceptance letter. Bob was pleased about this and I was grateful, for he had voiced reticence about going to a place often described as miraculous and mysterious. I noticed however, that he read with interest the books describing this 30-year-old community.

Chapter 21

SCOTLAND

 In and through community lies the salvation of the world.

M. Scott Peck

The morning of February 26, 1992, we arrived in Glasgow, Scotland. Despite jet lag, we rented a car and drove to Oban, sightseeing on the way. We were not expected to arrive at Findhorn until the 29th, so had three days on the western coast while heading north. It was the start of a love affair with this magnificently rugged country.

On Saturday we left our car in Inverness and boarded the train for an all-too-brief ride to Forres, where we would be picked up by bus and taken to Findhorn. We were scheduled to stay at the park where Eileen, Peter and Dorothy originally had demonstrated their faith in God's word in the early 60's. Now this spot was but one locale among many in the area where people came from around the world to attend experience weeks, stay on to study and work, or participate in one of hundreds of sessions being offered on a myriad of planetary, spiritual and social topics.

Our bus wound its way through the town of Forres and onto the Findhorn Peninsula which juts into the North Sea and Firth of Forth. The words of Paul Hawken circled dizzily in my head and I revisited the sense of wonder I had felt when I read the first paragraphs of his book, *The Magic of Findhorn.*

There have been stories in the press and other media about a small community in the north of Scotland called Findhorn where people talk to plants with amazing results — stories of vegetable and flower gardens animated by angelic forms...stories of plants performing incredible feats of growth and endurance: 40-pound cabbages, 8-foot delphiniums, and roses blooming in the snow — all a short distance from the Arctic Circle...people heard talking to plants and angels in a casual and informal way, creating a Garden of Eden where only gorse bushes and spiky grass grew before; a cold windblown peninsula jutting into the North Sea with soil as sandy and worthless as your local beach; a community said to be run and operated under messages and guidance received from God through Eileen Caddy, the wife of...Peter Caddy.

I had reveled in this tale of endurance, faith and outright miracles. The community had experienced many changes since Hawken's book was

published in 1975, and the only one of the three
original founders remaining there today is Eileen.
Dorothy Maclean left for the states in the 70's,
after years of experiencing profound messages
from spirits from the Kingdom of Nature. Peter
had eventually left Eileen and the Findhorn community as well to continue his journey in new environs. But many others had gathered in the mean-
time and the community now totaled about 150
members living in the original park and in the
Cluny Hotel in Forres. While 40-pound cabbages
and 8-foot delphiniums are no longer grown, gardens of beauty continue to abound and *The
Findhorn Garden,* a book published by the
Findhorn Foundation states:

*Findhorn proclaims the image for humanity
of a new maturity, the birth of the consciousness
of participatory divinity, of co-creation with
God...Whether you tend a garden or not, you are
the gardener of your own being, the seed of your
own destiny...the principles involved go far beyond gardening and embrace all activities of life.*

We were to join 17 other people from around
the world for this session. Upon arrival we walked
into the original dining hall in the park, now thirty
years in existence, and were warmly greeted by
our group leaders Maria and Sabine. Our roommates, Inga and Russell, were a pleasant couple

from Scotland, and we were soon comfortably sharing stories of our lives in the cozy living room of our cottage.

The week was aptly named. "Experience Week" was packed with experiences: We toured, discussed, gardened, performed sacred dance, learned, shared, meditated in sanctuary, and worked. We ate well, slept well, studied, challenged one another, experienced discord, experienced elation, and experienced the mystical within ourselves and each other.

As I danced I felt lighter and more fluid. As I walked the grounds I connected deeply with the earth under my feet and with the fellow pilgrims all around me. As we shared I learned to listen and honor the diversity among us. As we ate we talked excitedly about our lives and drew closer.

One memorable morning we were all in the Great Hall in the dance studio behind the stage area, and we were each asked to become a planet. The instructor asked us to put on blindfolds. Then she began playing a hauntingly beautiful piece of music and said we were to orbit the room but never touch another planet, for we were all alone in our particular path. We moved to the music for several minutes. It truly did feel lonely. Then she asked us to link up with one other planet and orbit the room together. This felt better. Then we were asked to orbit in groups of four and finally to become one single group of planets linked in the same system and moving as one. When the music finished, and we removed our blindfolds, I was looking up into the eyes of my husband.

On Monday we joined others at our chosen work sites and discovered that workers start the day by sharing their answer to the question "How are you?" while standing in circle together. This is followed by the focalizer's meditation. The focalizer is in charge of focusing the tasks at that particular work site. However, the focalizer was not to be thought of as a supervisor. We were all to approach the tasks as equals. It was sweet indeed for the work went swiftly and smoothly. Bob and I agreed that this approach needed to be brought to the farm.

We studied the organization and daily inner-workings of this community. Bob spent hours in the library, a place he felt most comfortable, where he researched the history and ideas behind Findhorn Foundation. We learned the meaning of attunement, a meditation method for hearing the clarity of one's inner voice or Higher Self and sharing it with others, who in turn shared their inner wisdom as well.

We were privileged to witness the entire community meeting together in the Great Hall one evening. This meeting occurs only once every two years, and involves everyone attuning at the same time to make a decision affecting the community for the next two years.

The task of the community was to attune to the eight individuals who would serve as the core group for the community. Once this group was established, these people would be the spiritual focalizers for the entire community. Eileen was automatically a member. The others being considered had selected themselves out of an original group of some twenty people. Many rounds of attunement had already taken place in sanctuary and this was the final round with all community members now invited.

The people chosen through attunement to be the slate of eight sat in chairs placed on the arena stage so all could see. When we entered the hall Maria directed us to sit in the side section. It started out much as a regular meeting would start. A focalizer spoke of the task at hand and, after introducing us as visitors, let each "candidate" give a brief presentation to those gathered. When presentations were complete, the entire auditorium went into absolute silence for many minutes. I marveled at the intensity I felt in this large space filled with people from all around the world. What were the inner voices like that spoke to each of them? Or did they hear a single voice as I did? Was it different for each person seated there? Whatever the case, what bound us all together in that space that evening felt timeless and boundless. Was it the same feeling for all, I wondered.

As we sat in the silence I envisioned what the world would be like if governments and organizations and diverse communities of people joined together in this manner daily, weekly and monthly to make decisions. Then I was reminded of the strife in the world at large, seemingly so distant at the moment; and how relatively noisy people become when they gather, unless in a holy space. The deep and spiritual parts of our lives seem to be completely separate from the daily issues, I realized. And I felt sadness.

The voice of the focalizer cut through my thoughts. She asked if there were any objections to the slate of eight. There were none. It was decided.

Maria pointed out to us later that the lack of dissention was unusual, and had there been some, the meeting would have continued until a full attunement had been reached. This is similar to the method used by the Quakers, who call it consensus.

We discovered that the community had built a beautiful home for Eileen in the original park very close to the small green caravan that once housed her, Peter and their three children, with a lean-to tacked on for Dorothy. I had hoped that Eileen would be present when we visited, for I feel a deep attraction to her. But I was told that she had gone for the winter months and was not expected back.

On Tuesday morning, as community members and visitors in attendance were about to begin twenty minutes of silent meditation Eileen slipped into sanctuary. I felt strength in her presence and gave thanks for receiving such strength simply by sharing space and a purpose with her and the others.

Bob and I felt, in retrospect, that we gave birth to the center that week. All of our Findhorn Experience Week colleagues agreed to support us in that thought. I gave a small candle to each of our group members on the last day and committed to writing to everyone when we knew the exact day of the cleansing and blessing ceremony at the farm. We planned to hold a simple ceremony prior to moving there. We would light our candles at precisely the same time, we agreed, in honor of this new center being brought to reality. The knowledge that candles would be lit all over the world was strengthening.

I had many times during the week felt inadequate, unworthy and just plain dumb around the history and power and depth of this unique community. It came as a great surprise to me when my roommate Inga, on the final day of farewells, shared her first impressions of me. She said she had seen me walk into the dining hall that first morning and had decided that I was strong and powerful and she wanted nothing to do with me. "But I knew you would be our roommates," she said, "and sure enough, they called us to be together." Then she smiled across the circle and added, "I just want you to know that I'm really glad now that you were my roommate."

Bob also brought tears to my eyes when he said his formal goodbyes to the circle by stating, "I am not where many of you are, spiritually. But someday I hope to be. I hope to experience all that you have experienced and more."

Packed and ready to leave on Saturday morning, we loaded up our little rental car which Bob had retrieved from Inverness. We were scheduled to fly home five days later so had plenty of time to explore Scotland further and reflect together upon the week we had just experienced.

Saying goodbye to the members of our group was very difficult. We had spent intense days together and I felt deeply connected in myriad ways. Some of us had shared stories of our spiritual journeys. Others had shared family sorrows. We had all been challenged to go deeper and to look at ourselves, and our life purposes. We had opportunities to learn and be challenged by members of the Findhorn Community. The work sites had been filled with invaluable lessons. And over pints at the local pub in Findhorn village, we had bonded in our laughter and storytelling. Each diverse person from unique points on the globe had contributed gifts to the group. It was community, and it felt good.

As we drove out of the park to head south along the coast, I clutched a candle that Mary, a group member from England had given us. It was a golden candle from the Phoenix Center at Findhorn. She had gifted us with it that we might use it during the lighting ceremony on the farm.

"Dearest Mary, Dearest Mair. Dearest Crystal and Russell and Inga. Thank you. Travel with us Richard and Annette and Gerry," I prayed. "Lisa, Raija and Howard, give us your blessings. Help us carry the load, dear Michael and Michael and Mark and Sharon. And thanks be to Sabine and Maria for your wisdom and service as focalizers to us all."

Such were my thoughts as we pulled out of the park and drove down the road. Soon our journey and the rain soaked countryside caught my attention and I felt renewed excitement for what lay ahead.

Chapter 22

A GIFT OF HEALING

 People have tended to believe that the universe was small and limited. They believed that reality is that which is visible and tangible. Now modern science would indicate that reality is the invisible, the intangible, the things that are incomprehensible.

Sir John Templeton

One event during Findhorn week changed my view of life forever. It was an encounter with the spirit of a deceased loved one. It wasn't the first time I had experienced a spirit, but certainly the most dramatic encounter.

On Tuesday morning, I was toweling myself dry after a shower when suddenly I became intensely aware of my mother, as if she were standing behind me. She had died ten years earlier, almost to the day. Shivers ran down my spine but it was a brief episode and I soon dismissed it.

The following day the entire group assembled at Cluny Gardens in nearby Forres. This is the grounds of an enormous old hotel now owned by Findhorn and the site of many events. We were aerating the grounds, all nineteen of us, jumping up and down on pitchforks, in a long line, laughing and singing and thoroughly enjoying the mutual task.

My abdomen began to hurt and the pain increased as the minutes went by. I mentioned it to Mair, one of the women with whom I had previously shared. She stopped abruptly and said, "Lie down on the grass, over there out of the way. I'll give you a hand."

As Mair put her hand on my belly she said, "Just start talking. Where is this pain coming from? What is it saying to you?"

I immediately remembered my mother's presence in the bungalow. I felt a deep desire to talk about her, to explain what happened, to affirm her presence in my life. Mair said, "I'm listening."

In March of 1982 I had received a call that my mother was unexpectedly ill. I made arrangements to visit her, but because I was flying from the Virgin Islands to Arizona, the trip was delayed until after Easter. The doctor confirmed this was no problem. "Whatever it is, it's not life threatening," he said, from three thousand miles away. On Easter Saturday I received another call from mother's close friend, Tom, who said she was in a coma and I must come immediately.

I barely made it to her side. Once there I was confronted with a decision to either order "heroic measures" or disallow them. The same doctor sat in the waiting room at 2 a.m. explaining to me that my mother was already in a coma and that it had done significant damage. He gave little hope. I asked him why this was happening, what had gone wrong? He said he didn't know. Reluctantly I had asked that there be no resuscitation.

Four hours after my arrival Mother died. In contrast to the peace I felt when Dad had died two years earlier after a lingering illness, her death was very difficult for me. We were just beginning to get beneath the surface of our relationship, to grow closer. She had begun to open herself up after my father's death, and I wanted to share in this transformation.

I felt cheated by God that day. Mother had never revealed to me her deepest self until something started to surface in those last two years. Had she ever truly known herself? Had she lived a fulfilling life as a wife, mother and church musician? I wanted to know these things, to understand her. To appreciate her.

She was a very bright and beautiful woman, valedictorian of her high school class, with musical talents well above average. She had been offered a four-year scholarship to Julliard School of Music. This was in the days, however, when many felt women went to college primarily to find a husband and to be prepared in case they were ever left a widow. "Women's primary responsibility," my grandmother once said, "is to serve their husbands." Hence it had made no sense to my North Dakota grandparents that their daughter be whisked off to the East Coast. Better she become a music teacher, and for that she only required a degree from Valley City State Teacher's College.

Two years after graduation Lois met Mac. She later described him as the least handsome man she ever met, but one of the finest as well. She had seen the gift my father had for loving, for reaching out a hand in friendship to all those he met. We both delighted in his incorrigible sense of humor, one more than likely from the McCleary Irish bloodline. I shared his passion for sports and sportsmanship, occasionally attempting to be the son he never had. This accounted for my tomboy approach to life as a youngster which stayed with me into adulthood. Dad was my own personal Jimmie Durante, complete with a keen intellect and a caring heart. In many ways, he was my best friend.

What Mother did not recognize at the beginning of their relationship was Dad's inability to handle alcohol and his propensity for imbibing frequently. It didn't take long for reality to set in. He got drunk their wedding night. His cronies had shown up at their honeymoon cabin and he stayed outside with them until the wee hours of the morning. She spent the night alone. Although I had been around Mac's drinking, I first heard this story after 40 years had passed. She told it to me the week Dad died, the same week I witnessed a dramatic change in her relationship with me and with the world. As if for the first time she was free.

But too late, it seemed. The prior years had taken their toll. Stridency had already replaced her innate gentleness. Life was to be controlled. Dad and I had to succeed in her stead. She tried to live through us, busily innovating ways to keep Dad sober and keeping me on the path to success. But success was defined by Lois. She wanted us to be worthy of being her family, and the opinions of others seemed to matter more to her than did our own.

She was frequently disappointed. And while she taught me strength and stamina, I felt it came at the cost of intense judgementalism. It was from my father that I learned unconditional love.

Dad seemed to find little reason to be judgmental, but always had a knack for challenging me to be better, to choose more wisely. His arms were there to give a pat on the back or a push on the swing. All through the years of my growing, he saw the need for balance between himself and my mother, with me in the middle, and I believe he wanted me to feel safe.

After the cancer, when I was forced to examine my relationship with Mom, I had finally begun to see her from another point of view. I had learned about co-dependency and could imagine what it must have been like to give up the very core of her being and live through others. I finally was able to understand a sense of pride and honor within her that I had never recognized before. I knew that her love was there, but blocked by the demands of her family and society; blocks that she saw as very real.

As I let these thoughts flow out to the Scottish countryside and the listening ears of Mair, the pain in my belly subsided. Mair said, "You have a lot of grieving here. The fact that you felt her presence is significant. We have a free afternoon tomorrow. Find someone at the Park to help you follow up on this." After thankful hugging we returned to our pitchforks and the Cluny countryside.

The following morning while working in the kitchen, Carmella, a colleague in carrot cutting from Monday morning, walked through the kitchen. She had shared with me that her insightfulness and intuitive capacity had significantly increased in the past year at Findhorn. She had been gifted with the ability to help heal others, she said, and described herself as a psychic healer. I called out her name and she walked over. We agreed to meet in our bungalow at three.

Carmella walked into the living room, settled herself in a nearby chair, and I began by describing my experiences thus far. She asked, "Is there some reason why your mother would be sad?" I said yes, and shared much of what I had shared with Mair.

Carmella paused, then said, "Diane, I don't know how to tell you this, except to say that your mother is here." I swallowed hard. "Good," I said. "Let's get on with it."

She asked that I sit in the center of the living room, facing whichever wall I found attractive. I chose the fireplace wall where an original painting hung; my mother had at one time studied watercolors. As I focused on the painting, Carmella spoke from behind me. She explained that she was doing a cleansing and prayer in preparation and that I should be still and relax.

In the quiet that followed, the door to the living room, shut tightly by Carmella, opened. Carmella uttered a short gasp. "Welcome," she said. She explained that my mother had entered the room, appearing to her as a white sunburst-shaped spirit. "Close your eyes please," she said to me.

Carmella shut the door. It opened again. She left it open and said, "Your mother wants it understood that she will leave when this is over. The door symbolizes her intentions. And she will truly be leaving this time."

I said I understood, but I wondered if that meant my mother had been stuck in the earth plane all these years. Had she hung around all this time because of unfinished business? Was I the reason? I was deeply moved by this possibility.

I remembered an incident at the hospital six months after her death. I had flown to Delaware from the Virgin Islands for a complete hysterectomy. Had mother had similar surgery during her final illness, she might still have been alive. So as I was rolled into surgery I glanced upward and whispered, "This one's for you, Mom."

During my recovery, flowers arrived from Bob in the Virgin Islands. His card read: "See you in St. John. Love, Mom." I laughed aloud at this cosmic touch. When I asked the florists about it they said that there was static on the line as the message was given and this was what they thought they heard. "How delightful," I had mused. But in those days it had seemed merely a bit of coincidence.

Carmella said, "Your mother is directly in front

of you now. You are free to silently speak with her."

She explained that my mother was asking me to share with her whatever it was that I wished to say. My mind was a jumble of thoughts. I concentrated my energies behind closed eyelids but no words came. Carmella spoke from behind me. "She can't understand what it is you are saying."

I said aloud, "That's because I'm totally confused as to what to say. My mind is a mess of over 40 years of our relationship." Carmella asked me to try again.

I paused, and then mentally asked my mother what it was that she needed from me. Instantly, deep within me, I knew the answer. She wanted my forgiveness.

Calmly and silently I sent words of complete forgiveness to her and told her, "Mom, you were exactly who and what I needed for the lessons I needed to learn. I forgive you and I love you. I release you now, and I wish you to release me so I can also move on." I sat expectantly awaiting a reply. None came.

"She's leaving now. I will walk with her out to the gardens," Carmella said.

My heart caught in my throat, and I struggled not to cry. Suddenly I was enveloped in a palpable feeling of love that wrapped me in a cocoon of warmth. I felt peace-filled and safe. The tears rolled down my cheeks as I was overcome with tenderness.

Carmella paused at the door and said, "Diane, do you feel the love in this room?" I tearfully acknowledged her with a silent nod, my head bowed forward.

As Carmella left the room, I opened my eyes in time to see a light leave as well. The room became significantly dimmer and the door closed.

Carmella returned as I was dabbing my nose with a tissue. She complimented me on my strength and said, "Your mother is going to hang around the gardens for a few minutes and then she's headed up to a distant star for two of three years of preparation. Who knows, she may return as a grandchild." I laughed at the thought, thoroughly enjoying the possibility, although I wondered whether the distant star was a metaphor or an actuality.

I told Carmella that I thought my mother had just given me the greatest gift of our lives. She agreed, and added, "You are now operating at a new and higher level. I need to do some work with you to prepare you for what is to come. Are you willing?"

During the next hour Carmella told me that my mother had appeared to me at this time because it was a safe space for both of us and, more importantly, because I was ready to forgive her. I had finally learned to walk in her shoes, to look at her life from her perspective and not from mine.

Carmella asked, "Are you willing?" I answered, "Willing to do what?" "Your life's work," she replied.

I said yes. She repeated the question a second time. I answered yes again. She repeated a third time. I repeated my answer.

"Well done," she said. "When the guidance asked me to respond to that question, they didn't believe me until the twenty-first time!"

"What guidance?" I queried.

Carmella explained that she had been responding to her guidance at the time just as I was now responding to mine. "You are now working with seven guides, which," she said, "is what you had asked for." I was so intrigued I forgot to ask her when, where and how I had made such a request. But I remembered thinking that it must have been prior to my birth.

Carmella also taught me a cleansing and grounding ritual. She explained that I would one day be working with others who were ill or out of balance and would need to keep my feet on the ground and my self clear of others' influences during the work. I was to stand tall, with arms outstretched and invoke the cleansing by saying: "By the power of the Christ Light within me, I cleanse and bless my body and my soul."

She also explained that I could invoke the same Christ Light to cleanse and bless others as well. She said she used this whenever she was to work with another. It assisted in staying clear of another's pain or illness. "And it keeps our feet on the ground even though we are intuitively connected to the above," she added.

Carmella concluded, "It's a privilege to work with you, Diane." She then promised me a future of challenges and closed by saying that she had been told I would do similar healing work to hers.

"After this afternoon, I doubt if anything will be too surprising," I exclaimed. But secretly I was highly doubtful of Carmella's forecast. My psychic abilities were minimal compared to hers and I had never healed anyone that I knew of. My stomach had to hurt before my own mother could get my attention. And I certainly did not relish a lifetime of pain in order to be contacted by the other realm. I said goodbye to Carmella feeling exhausted and peaceful but remaining skeptical.

Much later that evening I began to digest what had happened. I had shared everything with Bob, who was deeply moved. Then I remembered the card I had drawn on my first day at Findhorn, when we were each asked to draw a card from a brightly decorated deck containing 52 angels. Each angel's identity was unique: Peace, Openness, Love, Transformation, Grace.... I received the angel of Spontaneity. The others chuckled at my receiving a quality so immediately obvious in my personality. Now I knew why this angel had come.

The universe had opened its windows and doors to me in ways I had never before experienced, and my spontaneous responses had been my contribution to the process. Miracles seldom are expected nor are we "ready" for them when they do appear. Drawing this angel had taught me that blindwalking in spontaneity is fundamental to learning, growing and being able to be present within each precious moment.

Chapter 23

LESSONS IN PATIENCE

 ...There is no room for doubt nor is there room for compromise. It all seems impossible in many ways but the hurdles have mostly been crossed because true hurdles exist in the mind, not in the illusory world. You hear clearly and well today. You feel our power within you and the fusion of All Power brings miracles. Let us go forward in complete faith.
Message, May 21, 1992

Winter still covered our end of Lake Superior when we returned home in mid-March. I was convinced that the house would be sold soon, but there were no leads. Bob began questioning my vision, and I was hard pressed to tell him with any certainty how we could afford to buy the farm.

Even after the enormous impact of Findhorn and my mother's visitation, it was still very possible for my shadow side to dominate; I was down in the dumps more often than not. It was a daily struggle to overcome fear and doubt.

I wrote and rewrote budgets based upon the house sale. We talked less about the farm each day, although each of us secretly drove down

McKinley road every so often just to be near the land and the buildings. If it hadn't been for the messages always offering love and support, I would have truly begun to lose faith. But the voice was persistent. And each day I would once again affirm my dedication to the idea of the center.

I had by now become accustomed to Franklin and Spirit Woman as two identities from the realm of spirit. They had meanwhile been joined by others in what I saw as the circle of seven. The newer entities had their place in the circle but their identities remained unclear. Since the voice seemed to be a unified voice for God rather than any particular guide, I felt comfortable not knowing their identities, although on infrequent occasions Franklin would sign a message.

Two years earlier a singular messenger had appeared, however. While on the phone with a fellow student of the Course I heard my colleague say, "When Helen died of cancer...." I quickly interrupted, "Excuse me, are you talking about Helen Schucman who scribed the course?" Although I knew she had died, this was the first I had heard that it was from cancer. "That can't be," I insisted. "It can't be." The voice on the other end of the line confirmed that indeed it was so.

I recall putting down the phone and rushing upstairs to my office. I careened wildly on the stairs as I felt anger enveloping me. Slamming shut the door and looking heavenward I shouted, "How could you! How could you do that to me?! You heard the voice of Jesus directly, you wrote some of the most important words to be shared with mankind in two thousand years. I have based my healing on these words, the words of Jesus. I have said I am cured of cancer. How could you do this to me?!" I repeated over and over to Helen and to Jesus and to no one in particular. I collapsed in a heap of fear and rage.

I did not come downstairs until 2 a.m. By then I was exhausted from weeping and shouting and fighting back the fear that was building in the center of my being. As I lay next to Bob, who was sleeping soundly, I remember falling asleep to the litany of the words I had created in my head: "How could you? How could you? How could you?"

The next morning I awoke late and, after my morning coffee, went upstairs to try to regain balance and strength. Sitting at the word processor, I asked for guidance which I now routinely did as part of my morning ritual of prayer and meditation. My fingers touched the keys and for the first time, I heard an inner voice that sounded the same to me but was speaking in the first person:

"I was incorrect in believing that the messages and the voices could be other than what they said they were. It is clear on a different plane now and I do not wish the same result for yourself [on the earth-plane]. Do not be concerned with me as I chose that manner of exiting the world. It was all I could choose at the time. I see your agony as you wrestle with trust and say to you, you are indeed a Holy Child and all of you join as one in bringing peace to the world. Do not let anything get in the way of your journey to God for the world depends upon it. I did what I had to do in the earthly existence you are familiar with. I fulfilled the one thing I needed to fulfill. That is all that matters ultimately. Remember that. You too have a part in the plan and it will be fulfilled as you have prom-ised. So let the Christmas message come through and be within you ... Love is all there is. (signed) Helen, Nov. 27, 1990."

I sat back in my chair and breathed a deep sigh of release. I felt as I had when embraced by the love of my Mother at Findhorn. Not only was I filled with peace but I marveled at the immense sources of support available to each of us as we open to possibilities of unlimited union. It was the only time I have ever heard the voice who calls herself Helen. "Reality is the invisible, the intan-gible, the things that are incomprehensible," Templeton has said. Indeed.

Now, during this time of waiting two years

later, a third voice was joining in. I slowly realized I was communicating with an entity that professed to be Greta Potter, former mistress of the farm. This intrigued me and lifted my spirits. Greta would sometimes sing in a gentle and lilting voice. Sometimes she would share lines of poetry, or just give a simple and to the point message. She always sounded upbeat and very sure of herself.

Greta approved of our hopes and plans, and said she was a member of the seven who now worked with me. She cheered me immediately one day by sharing this: "Let us lighten up, my dear. This is getting to be a very dreary time for you and Robert and should not be so. The process is not over! You mope as if you are going to lose the farm. Can you possibly believe that? Take it from one who knows. You will be the stewards and it will all occur as it is meant. Go enjoy yourself. Make a potato salad, read, laugh, join your friends. Be alive in the moment. Enough of the other! (signed) Greta. May 24, 1992."

I picked up a pen of a different color and scrawled at the bottom of the page, "I release with giggles and love, Dearheart."

Chapter 24

SPRING AND RENEWAL

 Even miracles are mundane happenings that an awakened mind can see in a fantastic way...We must remember that everything is ordinary and extraordinary. It is our minds that either open or close.

Natalie Goldberg

By March 31, 1992, my patience had run out. I wrote a letter to the owners of the farm, asking them to consider a land contract for one year, during which time we could winterize the lodge for our housing and continue to seek a buyer for the house in Bayfield.

After much communication and deliberation, the Seagraves agreed. Bob and I were once again back on the path. The equity in our Bayfield house became the downpayment. We had by now realized that renting the Bayfield house and the farmhouse on the farm would be a solution to our financing problems. Within one day of these decisions, Kayci, a colleague of Bob's, walked up to Bob at work and expressed her interest in the Bayfield house should we ever want to rent it. Two days later, another acquaintance, Terry, called and said she had heard we were buying the farm, and would we consider renting the old farmhouse to her? We had not even had time to place an ad and both places were already rented. I was reminded of Emmet Fox's wisdom from so long ago:

"Whatever you may require to answer that call, will God provide. Money, opportunity, introductions, knowledge, training, freedom, leisure, strength and courage – all will He furnish if you be about His business and not your own."

The closing on the property was scheduled for the 27th of July. I wrote letters to our supporters from Findhorn and advised them that we would hold a cleansing and blessing ritual on August 1, with the lighting of the candle at three p.m. Bayfield time. I also proceeded with the establishment of a nonprofit organization to handle the business of the center.

Part of establishing a nonprofit is naming it. I had been making lists everywhere, brainstorming ideas on the back of book jackets, on napkins and legal pads. Bob and I would share ideas together but none of our ideas seemed to grab hold. When I asked for guidance I was not given a specific answer. Evidently this was in our hands.

The day finally came when I was to mail in the legal papers to the state of Wisconsin. Still no name. So I plucked out of nowhere "Hog Heaven, Inc." It came from a joke that Mel and I shared, a take off on Fun Hogs; we saw ourselves as Spirit Piggies about the vision of the center. The state application required a second choice; I wrote in "H.H. Inc." And a third choice. In frustration I wrote "Potter's Farm, Inc."

I couldn't believe the response: Hog Heaven and H.H. Inc. were both taken! So our official name was Potter's Farm.

Of course it is perfect. It honors Doc Potter who bought and created this space, and Greta, my dear colleague in spirit and poet-in-residence of Potter's Farm. Only later did a second meaning become clear to me. We are the clay in the Potter's hands, are we not? So the name Potter's Farm is quite right indeed; much in the same manner that Brander and Associates became such an apt title. It's all very simple when Spirit is in the lead.

PART FOUR

THE WEST
AND
BIRTH

Chapter 25

JOHN

 Your friends will know you better in the first minute you meet than your acquaintances will know you in a thousand years.

Richard Bach

It was July, a month before the move to Potter's Farm. I was turning the car onto Highway 2, about to come into the stretch I now referred to as Eagle Alley, and saw a hitchhiker standing alongside the road. The front seat was too full of books and tapes to pick up a rider so I passed him by. He nodded directly at me, then turned his face away. I knew in that instant his simple gesture had said, "Ah, a lone female driver. I understand." I immediately pulled over and stopped, scrambling to clear my books and tapes off the seat next to me.

He ran to the car, smiled through the window at me, and pulled open the door. He was average height, a fair-haired man with little evidence of sun upon his face. He appeared to be in his early forties but had a timeless face. Swinging a small knapsack off his back and placing it on the floor of the front seat, he climbed in and settled comfortably in the passenger side.

"Hi," I said. "I'm Diane."

"Hello. I'm John."

John's features fascinated me. He had a wide, innocent face, and a broad smile. His eyes were blue and deep. They twinkled. Either that or his face reflected the light of the day. His presence instantly cheered me. "No downcast moods for this one," I thought.

John thanked me for picking him up and remarked how unusual it was for a woman to do so. "You look honest," I said smiling. He said that his last ride had been with a Native American from a nearby reservation. He said they'd had a grand talk and he had gotten out at the waterfront park in Ashland.

He asked, "And what is it you do?" My usual response to this question is to go into detail about my business. But this time I felt it wasn't appropriate. I felt the desire to share more depth. "Well, my husband and I are moving onto a 50-acre farm west of Washburn next month," I said. "I'm starting a spiritual retreat center, a center for personal and social transformation."

"Washburn," he said. "That's the town I saw from the park. I was down on the shore and I had a vision of a piece of land above Washburn. It was lifted up, as if held by God's own hands. It was blessed and filled with light." I looked over at him. He was smiling. My heart began to race.

John shared with me stories about miracles and his witness of them in many parts of the country. He told of a young boy he had known who had died and was placed in the morgue for identification.

"I went to the morgue with his mother," John said. "She refused to believe that he was dead. She stood in that cold room with his body lying there and she prayed from the bottom of her heart for a miracle. I saw first hand what happened then. The lad sprang up from his pallet, I swear." John burst into laughter. "You should have seen the coroner fly out of the room and down the hallway!" We both laughed at his description of the poor man. "Can't say as I blame him," I added and we both laughed again.

I told John about the recent and sudden death of our neighbor, Greg, who had been a close friend and a supporter of the center. "He always joked that he would be the chef," I said. "He would serve oatmeal when people needed sustenance and prunes when they got stuck." We chuckled, and John said, cocking his head, "Greg will be of more help where he is, Diane." I looked over at John and wondered, who *is* this guy anyway?

We rode in silence for a few miles, until John said suddenly, "There is a very important corner of the land — the northwest corner of the farm, I believe...."

"That's where the pond is," I replied. "And the start of a path into the woods. It's really part of a circular meadow. I feel lots of power there." John nodded knowingly. He then added, "I've cleansed a lot of land by walking the land with the owners."

"John," I asked, "will you come and walk our land with us? You seem to understand this so well. Bob and his mom and I are going to do a cleansing and blessing ritual on August first, but I would love to have you visit sometime and assist as well." John said he would.

We reached Duluth and the downtown corner where he was to depart. He said he worked as a waterfront counselor for sailors in Michigan. But he didn't have a card or an address. I gave him my card and he promised to write. I said we would be on the farm in a month and would then arrange to have him visit.

As I touched him on his arm, really wanting to hug him, I said, "John, this has been a beautiful meeting. I am so moved by your presence. Please keep in touch."

"I promise I will," he said, clasping my hand.

I again stared at his eyes which I could only get glimpses of while I was driving. They were peaceful, kind and very direct. He looked back at me, then slid out of the car, shouted a final thanks and closed the door.

I had to share this experience with someone. I kept repeating out loud, "Thank you, thank you, thank you." I raced up the hill to the airport and called Brenda.

"You are not going to believe what just happened to me," I exclaimed. "I was driving down that same stretch of highway where I met Eagle...."

Chapter 26

RITUAL OF LOVE

 Forget not once the journey is begun the end is certain. Doubt along the way will come and go and go to come again. Yet is the ending sure. No one can fail to do what God appointed him to do. When you forget, remember that you walk with Him and with His word upon your heart.

A Course in Miracles

I awoke on August first to bright bold sunlight and stretched my hand across the coverlet to grasp Bob's hand. Staring around the room that was now our bedroom, I thought, "What memories!" All those years of this space being my second floor office. This is where Brander and Associates began five years ago. This is where the cancer was faced and where prayers and professional work have existed side by side all these years. This is where the Associates have come to me for so very long now. This is where Grandmother Full Moon first shined down on me as I gazed out the window the evening of my arrival. It felt as if She were calling my name.

Now my office and personal space were downstairs in the back of the house. The orange shag carpet and orange walls had been replaced with muted earth tones, giving the room a feeling of serenity. "Not for much longer," I thought.

We picked up Jean at her Bayfield apartment and drove out to the farm, our farm, at noon. I had been there earlier in the week to plan the ceremony. All the buildings were empty now, and seemed to be waiting for what was to come.

The stone mantle was filled with candles: one for all those who had come before us, one for the Potters, one for the Seagraves, one for all other life that dwells on the farm in whatever form, one for us and finally, the center candle, the golden candle from Findhorn, for the Creator and the farm itself. This candle we would light at exactly three P.M. our time to coincide with our colleagues from Findhorn.

We brought three folding chairs into the living room, then a small portable table. On it we placed a bouquet of flowers from the front garden and three crystal glasses. The tiny champagne bottle was put in the freezer to quick-chill and snacks went in the refrigerator. We would be hungry after the walk through all of the buildings.

I looked expectantly at Bob and Jean. "Are you ready?" They nodded agreement and we began our smudging and blessing ceremony in the lodge. Once the smudge bowl was lit and passed through the building, it was left to smolder and we shared the words:

"By the power of the Christ light within me, I cleanse and bless this lodge. Let this lodge be filled with light and with love. Let God dwell here and let us serve God's holy purpose in the name of Potter's Farm. Amen."

We walked slowly from building to building repeating this invocation in each, then gathered under a tall, strong birch at the entrance to the meadow. Bob threw tobacco and Jean cast corn-meal as I addressed the four directions: "Greetings to the East, space of the Rising Sun where Eagle flies and Illumination and Birth occur. Greetings to the South, the green place of Summer, of lushness flowering and growing through the Scrutiny of Mouse and Trickster Coyote. Greetings to the West, the time of Autumn, letting go, Introspection, Raven and Bear. Greetings to the North, the white place of Winter and Wisdom, Clarity, Buffalo and Owl." We then shared readings from Brooke Medicine Eagle's book, *Buffalo Woman Comes Singing.*

Bob read a prayer written by Francis of Assisi. He pledged our stewardship of this land by making a covenant with Creator: "We will celebrate the land and lake surrounding us, working in harmony with Spirit to co-create a place of beauty and depth befitting the tasks at hand."

It was nearing three when we returned to the lodge. I added one last candle to the mantle in memory of Greg, and began lighting all the candles. At exactly three we lit the center candle and stood in silence in front of the multiple, dancing flames. Somewhere in other parts of the world, perhaps in Findhorn, other candles were being lit to add to the Universal Light we were kindling here.

We shared a final reading from the *A Course in Miracles*, uncorked the split of champagne and toasted the joy that was in each of our hearts. "Here's to coming home," I said. "Welcome, welcome home!" We all had tears in our eyes.

Chapter 27

THE MOVE

 Okay, God. I know you have a really funny sense of humor, but I don't understand this one at all!

Marlo Morgan

August 1992 was filled with boxes and packing and all of the details of an uprooting. We were amazed at how much we had managed to accumulate in five years since sailing back into the Bayfield harbor. On August 20th the moving van arrived and we prepared to say goodbye to the neighborhood and the town where we had spent many years of our life.

The community of folks in the neighborhood had become very precious to us. We had shared laughter and tears with Greg and Betty; become close friends with Lauri, Sean and their three delightful children; swapped house renovation stories with Chuck, Tom and Barb; listened with delight to Milly's tales of the old days; and shared neighborhood barbecues and pot lucks which often included an even larger group. Our front porches were always scenes of spontaneous interaction which usually led to further fun. It was authentic community.

Greg's sudden death had preceded our leave-taking by two months. I shall always remember standing in the middle of the street on moving day, arms wrapped around Betty, mingling our tears as we said goodbye, layers of grief surrounding the move to the farm.

The work to be done became uppermost in Bob's mind upon arrival at the farm. We had three months at the most in which to convert a three-season lodge into a four-season home. Bob became reclusive by the end of the first day and by day three was hardly speaking to me. I was not only exhausted but sad, since I had pictured such a different beginning. Sunday I took a walk in the woods to regain my equilibrium.

When I returned, feeling much more centered, I noticed a stalk of roses growing by the front door, a single stem with four pink buds. My favorite number. My favorite flower. I decided it was a gift from the Cosmos and carefully picked it for my new office space in the lodge. As I brought the vase into the office and placed it on my desk, I noticed a pile of mail that had collected since moving day. On the top of the pile was a handwritten envelope from John. I was elated.

This is what I read, exactly as written:

Mr and Mrs. Branders;

Diane;

Peace, love and joy to all!

This letter I hope will find all of you well. a few short lines to let you know I am fine...and to open communications with you. I thank you again for your help to me!

Your real estate business was coming to a close when I saw you, did all go well...I have sent you both much support during that time "knowing" momentary "stress" always passes!

Thought, meditation, prayer have gone into the events that I "<u>saw</u>" in the period prior to me meeting you.

"<u>Knowing</u>" that all these events (my vision; your helping hand) were a "<u>participatory experience</u>" these are my reflections;

I. I saw "clearly" without doubt!

    a. from Ashland park a large section of land (many acres) totally within its entirety

        1. "<u>Lifted up</u>" as "<u>being raised</u>" <u>literally above its surroundings!</u>

        2. toward the heavens an anointing of this land.

        3. a positive, spiritual stronghold for love, peace, joy, Healing much more!

    b. a powerful testimony of things to come concerning this land and its future.

Reminds me of a Hebrew phrase "and I will raise you up and establish you as a star in the heavens! Jehovah's promise to David!"

c. I literally saw the entire property raised up (the thickness of the hand (depth) was very deep) as it was elevated and blessed!

As if "God's hand" had torn it away from its very earthly "roots" and raised it heavenward.

d. This land will never be the same again. I saw this prior to the time we met on highways 63/2, approximately one hour and twenty minutes. Something I thought about later. I had walked out of the park and had this "strong compelling drive" to go back. When I walked back to where I was originally standing, the vision came!

I am only to say this

1. I am at your disposal for whatever needs you may have.

2. I am open to communicate with you by phone or letter or whatever is convenient for you!

3. your kindness and your touch before leaving blessed me. I felt a healing! This meeting was not only for the "vision" and your encouraging concerning the sale of the property but was also a healing for me!

Your reply and love will be eagerly awaited and I assure you all things and more than you can imagine will come to pass for each of you.

yours always in Christ

John

I immediately wrote a response to this unusual man, in care of a Duluth address that was on the envelope.

I waited for two months for a reply to my letter. I then called Brenda and asked if she could find the location of the address. She reported that it was a Christian mission in Duluth. She said she asked about John but was given little information other than that he had been there. I called the mission and was told that he had indeed stayed there briefly, and yes they remembered he received a letter from Bayfield. Soon after that he had disappeared without a trace. "It was a little strange," the woman said, "because he seemed so friendly."

I pondered all of this over the next several months and came to accept that John had lost interest after I had written. I was sad but I eventually resigned myself to never seeing him again.

Chapter 28

BRANDER MEETS ASSOCIATES

 The Holy Spirit abides in the part of your mind that is part of the Christ Mind. He represents your Self and your Creator, Who are one. He speaks for God and also for you, being joined with both. And therefore it is He who proves them one. He seems to be a voice, for in that form He speaks God's Word to you. He seems to be a Guide through a far country, for you need that form of help. He seems to be whatever meets the needs you think you have.

A Course in Miracles

Fall on Potter's Farm was busy with professional work, farm work, and more farm work. Brenda and Don came to pile firewood one weekend and generally helped us get ready for winter. Their presence was good for our sagging spirits. But by late fall I had landed in the hospital with a strained back and while there was diagnosed with a hernia and ulcer. Seems that fear was busy working in my mind, thus my body.

Throughout the winter months we were severely tested. The temperature on Christmas Day was 52 degrees in our living room. We had stressed our bank account, our physical selves, and our spirits to the maximum. And still the house in Bayfield hadn't sold.

Once again, if it hadn't been for the messages and the power of this farm, I believe I would have truly lost faith in the entire project. But the messages just kept coming and continued to be filled with love and encouragement. How could I doubt? In the midst of such love, I couldn't.

In the spring I had a long breakfast with Marilyn Larson, a friend and Board of Trust member of Potter's Farm. Marilyn spoke easily of her guide, Sophie. I asked her how she learned her guide's name and she said simply, "I asked." I decided to do the same at the next opportunity.

That occasion came the following week when I was home alone. I seated myself at the dining table, and gazed through the picture window that framed the yard and trees near the lodge. As I relaxed and mulled it over, it seemed best to visualize the seven guides as if in a half-circle seated around the table with me.

First I smudged, then centered and grounded myself so I would be properly cleansed and prepared. After a brief prayer asking for safety and success I then relaxed in the chair, closed my eyes and pictured myself seated exactly where I was but in my mind's eye only. I decided I would start with those I already knew.

I took a deep breath and turned to Franklin who had appeared to me in the visioning at Open Space. He was exactly as I remembered him, dressed in casual clothes and wearing an Eagle mask. Next to him I saw Spirit Woman who had joined us that day as well. She was faint and a wispy white, and she radiated a surprising warmth. Next I turned to see Greta. She appeared as a smiling, middle-aged feminine presence, filled with joy and energy. She brought great certainty to the group. "Well, dear one," she seemed to be saying, " it's about time you took this step." She had a peaceful countenance and wore the same plain dress and hat, as in the only photograph we have of her.

The centerpiece of the seven was an angelic being-of-light. At first I heard the name Sarah, but that didn't feel right. So I listened until I heard Seren, as in Seren-ity. That felt absolutely appropriate. She was powerful both in appearance and in intensity, her energy was tangible, and I found her beautiful to look upon. I thanked Seren for her connection with me. How am I doing this so clearly, so easily? I wondered. As if reading my thoughts Seren spoke in a soothing voice. "Your willingness to be open to us is all that is needed. Your imagination allows us to come in. We thank you for that."

I then turned in my mind's eye to an elderly-looking guide whose name, he said, was Jacob. He exuded wisdom and I sensed his link with the Ancients. We looked at one another for several seconds, and then I turned to the guide to Jacob's left.

I was jolted to the point of gasping. Seated there exactly as I remembered him was John, the hitchhiker. "Hello, he said, smiling. "I've been waiting to make contact with you. I know you felt I was human, and for a brief period of time I was, but this is who I truly am, and I am here to assist with all matters concerning the farm." I remembered Marilyn's advice. "Are you an angel?" I asked.

"Yes indeed," John replied, his eyes twinkling. I could not move. This being who appeared before me in my mind's eye was as real to me at this moment as he had been in the front seat of my car. I was looking into the same eyes as I had then, and at the broad smile of amusement. I must have looked incredulous.

I was both stunned and yet compelled to turn to the seventh entity. He was a large presence and sat in the shadows. He said simply, "It is not yet time to know who I am. When the time comes, you will know." I thanked them all profusely and came back to the room in utter amazement.

How could an angel be riding in my car? And writing me letters? Who was the ancient one and why didn't he speak? Why wouldn't the last entity reveal himself? And the glorious being-of-light in the center of the semicircle, who was she and why did she exude such power? And where would Jesus be in relationship to all of this?

As I mulled over these questions, the answer to the final question became clear. "He is at the center of the circle," said a quiet voice within my being. "He is with you always."

I let all of the information gathered at this quest settle within me for several weeks. Then I decided to ask further by messaging. I heard:

"Regarding the lesson of hearing the inner voice...please hear this: The voice one hears on a daily basis is a voice for the Holy Spirit within. This voice is of a union of all voices and is the Voice for God, for All That There Is. From time to time there will be a special designation attached to a particular guide that wishes to be of assistance and this will occur when the voice identity is of a certain nature that it can be of help in that exact situation. Some of the guidance is of the angelic realm. Some is of a different history or makeup and would be referred to as a spiritual entity...one of your guides was recently a human on the earth plane but she was not what others might have thought. She met, married and stayed on Potter's farm in order to create the way for the coming events. That is why she is now in the guiding circle. She was totally human during that experience but has now returned to her place in the circle of light. The one identified as John was temporarily on the earth to relate to you in the experience of the move. This is to show the ways of God as wondrous indeed, as John traveled as an angel to be seated with you on the road. You must now be aware of Nakita who is of the earth in a spiritual way and of the wind and other spirits of the farm. [this refers to the unnamed guide who had not identified himself] His vibrations are felt from time to time. Franklin and Spirit Woman were the first to come, for they were the original guides who walked with you during the difficult years of childhood and adulthood when you were basically unaware of the help received or available to you. As an example, the car stayed on the road all those years ago because you let go of the wheel when you and Scott were facing certain death and thus allowed them to assist you. [this reference is to an near-accident that Scott and I experienced in 1970. The Volkswagen should have flipped over as it turned in circles on a freeway in Wisconsin. It remained upright and stopped in the left lane just as a semi whizzed by on the right.] That leaves Jacob and Seren. She is seated in the center of the seven. She is often the voice for all. Jacob has remained in the background and will continue to do so, for his purpose is of the Mindfulness and his wisdom is quietly there as needed. You will not notice his presence but he has been of the ancient ones with whom you worked in the beginning of time. Through his assistance he will help you to remember who you truly are.

"Your Associates are pleased to be identified as such. Remember though, that the guidance is always of the Holy Spirit and because your Brother, your Father/Mother and all the angels join together to bring help through all of the light workers, it is ultimately seen as one grand Whole. You are but a piece of the cosmic Truth yet all Truth is contained within you as a holy child of God. Help to teach this that others might leave behind their pain and join you in the truth of who they are as well."

The significance of the years of messaging became synthesized for me that day. The universe is indeed composed of mighty Companions in Spirit from many dimensions of being. Their assistance is wise, their ways are loving and they can guide us in manners both seen and unseen. But I also know that we are ultimately to believe in the power within us that is our heritage as God's children and we cannot forsake the earthly challenge that free will provides. Ultimately it is still up to each of us to choose between the voice for the ego or the voice for God. It is also our choice to respond in fear or to respond in love.

Chapter 29

A LOVING LESSON IN TIMING

 When you choose to do My will and walk in My ways, you have to do it whole-heartedly, no matter what it may mean. You have to take the rough with the smooth when learning that vital lesson of instant obedience to My will. Only when you give all will you receive all. In this spiritual life you cannot pick out all the plums and leave the cake; it is all or nothing. Many souls like to choose the parts in this life that appeal to them and to ignore those parts that do not comply with their baser desires. Doing so is not living a spiritual life...

Eileen Caddy

During our first winter the farm was a wonderland of beauty. Bob created a winding cross country ski trail through the woods that served as a walking trail during the rest of the year. When our spirits would sag we needed only to step into the crisp air and the breathtaking scenery to become both energized and peaceful once again.

The farm was working its way into our lives in many ways. For even though the lodge was not yet winterized, we were mesmerized by the beauty of the building and its strength of spirit. Our tenant Terry, a lover of the out-of-doors, joined with us in the rapture of this space and was deeply contented in the farmhouse. We often counted our blessings.

One issue kept niggling away in the back of my mind; the house in Bayfield *still* had not sold. Our land contract would be due in July and, even though my goal was to trust in God's plan in every respect, my old Control Self was busy imagining the worst. I could not conceive of why we were being punished for following every directive. Didn't God know that we needed to sell that house in order to buy the farm? What could this possibly mean? Throughout the spring and early summer my mind was cluttered with these fears, even though I knew that fear was my greatest hindrance and stood in the way of the walk of trust.

One day in exasperation, I asked for the umpteenth time for more specific guidance beyond being told to be patient and believe in the best outcome. I said, "I give up. I do not know what to do. The owners deserve to be paid as planned. We need to buy the farm. The Bayfield house hasn't sold. Please tell me, what are we to do?" I sat in silence and listened. The voice very clearly replied, "Go to the bank. Buy the farm."

"Excuse me?" I responded. The message repeated. I sat in silence. How can we do that? I thought. We don't have any more down payment other than what we've borrowed. We do have two rental incomes though....Maybe the rental incomes and the increase in appraised value due to our improvements would be enough to provide us with the loan? I sighed, "Okay, okay. I'll go back to the bank."

Within days the bank had approved our loan and at a much lower interest rate than we could have possibly received during our two years of waiting. We called the Seagraves and shared the good news. The closing date was set.

One week following the purchase of the farm, the house in Bayfield sold. The lesson from Creator was loud and clear: When you say you can't do something without certain conditions being met, you won't. You will instead put all sorts of limits on yourself, the situation and on your thinking. You will work yourself into a frenzy of fear and worry and fret. All for naught. Relax!

Chapter 30

PARTNERS IN GRACE

 When two or more are gathered in My name, there am I in the midst of them.

Jesus

In March of this same winter of 1993, I found myself one bleak spring day seated at the dining table thinking about the words that my daughter-in-law Ann, had spoken recently. "I don't know what's wrong with me," she had said. "I have a wonderful husband, a beautiful new son, and I feel like I want to die." Annie had suffered for almost five years from what the doctors had recently diagnosed as chronic fatigue syndrome. She was sick constantly, except for the months during the pregnancy. It was wearing on her and on Scott as well. I sensed her vulnerability and was very concerned.

I rose from the table and called Scott at his office in Helena, Montana. He and I have a remarkable directness with each other and I knew I could trust him to be honest with me. "Honey, I'm very concerned about Ann," I said.

"So am I, Mom," he replied.

I got to the point of my call. "Scott, would you support Ann in a visit to the farm? I don't know why but I feel its important for her to come here."

"You bet," he replied. "I'll support anything that might help. Please give her a call."

Ann agreed immediately and arranged to fly out in two weeks. But as I drove from Wisconsin to the Minneapolis airport, my mind was on my own daughter instead of Ann. Tara was two years younger than Scott but they had not always been raised in the same household during their childhood years. Wanting to be a liberated '60s woman, I had agreed to share the parenting when my first husband, Marshall, and I divorced in 1966. He had raised Tara while I had raised Scott during the school year and the children were usually with me each summer. Marshall and I maintained a strong friendship through this agreement.

But as I matured and the children grew older, this became an unhappy arrangement. I had become despondent over my daughter's absence from my life. When Tara was 13 and 14, she asked her father if she could live full time with Bob, Scott and me. He agreed and those two years were our happiest time together. But Marshall had eventually grown lonely and he asked Tara to return to California. Once again I was presented with the unthinkable.

In my grief and indecision I felt like the mother in *The Caucasian Chalk Circle*, who was asked to literally pull her child apart in order to prove her motherhood. I wanted Tara to stay. Her father wanted her with him. Tara could not be expected to choose between two parents whom she loved. So, after countless days and nights of angst and turmoil, I finally let go and she returned to live with her father.

I feel empathy for the many men in our society who love their children and have traditionally been asked to give them up. This appears to be changing, but there is never a good and right way to deal with the failures in our marriages and the vulnerable lives we bring into them. What are we to do? And what must it be like when anger and blame is the centerpiece of the family history — when communication is lacking from the start? Marshall and I have always been close friends which is a blessing.

Tara, her father, I and the rest of her family had recently experienced additional pain concerning her journey and her choices. As I drove toward the airport I knew that Tara must be allowed to travel her pathway, no matter how difficult, and that I would love and support her in that journey. How ironic, I thought, that I'm going to meet Ann at the airport, instead of Tara.

Ann and I spent the night in Minneapolis at my friend Kay's house, a great old house that was like a second home to me after all of the years of our friendship. Ann, Kay and I enjoyed one another thoroughly, savoring the evening like one savors a good bottle of wine. I was able to express the sadness I felt concerning Tara as Kay and Ann shored me up with love.

In the morning, Ann and I drove back to Wisconsin. I had not planned anything definite for us to do at Potter's Farm, but I shared with her that I would like to help her explore the illness. I suggested we first share in some readings and prayer together each morning. I felt a need for a studied approach to her blockages and issues, and proposed we use storytelling, drawings, and dialogue to explore her despair. "Would you also be willing to see Donna, a woman near the farm who does kinesthetic touch?" I asked. Ann replied simply, "I'm all yours. Whatever it takes, let's do it."

While driving, we listened to a tape of Melanie's. It was based on Marianne Williamson's book, *Return to Love*, a synthesis of *A Course in Miracles* in simple terms. As Ann listened to the tape she became animated and excited to get to work.

As we drove further and further north, Ann

shared that spirituality for her was at a dead-end. "I have nowhere to go," she confided. "God isn't real to me. It's as if nothing exists."

Ann had to fly home from Duluth on Tuesday. Sunday and Monday were all that we had. We worked together for two intense days, and by Monday afternoon we both felt that something had shifted in the spaces of our togetherness. Nebulous sorrow had somehow transformed to obvious joy, and Ann was on her way into a new life.

"Maybe," she had agreed, "it would be premature to leave the earth plane without discovering if there's another way to experience living here. Maybe, just because the way I've lived my life up til now has made no sense, that doesn't mean there isn't a way to live that makes perfect sense. Maybe I can go back to the beginning and start over, discarding the thoughts and belief systems that are unworkable and renew some of those which I've thrown out, such as my sense of adventure and my belief in the certainty of miracles. I'm beginning to feel once again the lure of the unknown, the power of imagination and a profound connection to God. Things I haven't felt since I was a child."

Ann later said that she had felt a heightened awareness while at Potter's Farm. "Prior to coming there, most events in my life were just coincidence, but after experiencing this awareness, I am looking at my life differently. Reality exists in a truer form at the farm and it has taught me plenty," she said.

We both experienced Spirit in unusual ways while she was there. The first night of our work, at about midnight, I was awakened by three sharp knocks on the bedroom wall. I came awake instantly and felt a strong presence in the room. It seemed to emanate healing energy within and all around me. My intuition told me that this presence was safe, so I silently welcomed it. Immediately the energy was vibrating within my body. It was exhilarating. After about two minutes, the presence left. I did not recall anything further, for the next thing I knew it was morning.

When I went to awaken Ann, she was sitting up in her bed and grinning. "At about midnight last night someone or something came through the entry to the lodge," she said, pointing to the door next to her bed. "A few minutes later it went by me again and left. No doors opened or closed, but all of the sounds were there." I told Ann of my experience at the other end of the house. We didn't know what to make of it, but agreed that this presence was a positive force.

"I also saw in my mind's eye," Ann said, "a procession in the woods near the meadow. Indians and horses. Three faces were very clear to me. They each wore skins on their head, but one wore Badger, one wore Bear and one Wolf. And the energy level was palpable." I nodded. "You never know what you'll find here, do you?" I observed. "The energy of this place feels ancient."

Monday evening, after our work together was done and, within earshot of Bob and me, Ann called Scott. "I'm healed," she said. I looked at her in amazement. She was stronger, more certain of herself, that I knew. But she was announcing something quite extraordinary. Like a miracle....

Ann's syndrome has never returned. As best we can explain it, we opened ourselves to being together in the name of all that is Good, True, and Infinite. We believe Ann opened herself to some painful memories and learned how she sabotaged herself out of the past, without even knowing it. We believe we also opened ourselves to the power of Love and the power of the farm as promised in John's letter. We realized that we believe God intends the very best for each of us if we will but ask and be open to receiving the answer.

I remember opening *A Course in Miracles* workbook on Ann's final morning on the farm and tearfully reading aloud that day's lesson:

"The light has come. You are healed and you

can heal. The light has come. You are saved and you can save. You are at peace, and you bring peace with you wherever you go. Darkness and turmoil and death have disappeared. The light has come."

Later Ann wrote: "I have begun seeking my new-found purpose. I want to find a way of living that exchanges hope for apathy, joy for sorrow, peace for anger, trust for guilt, faith for lies and love for fear....This then is where I am currently on my journey to what I once knew before I came here. It is not to an external place or person or goal out there somewhere. It is a journey within, at times blind and dark as I go back through my past. But the path shines with an ever increasing intensity now that I choose to see it. This is the light in the darkness, the place that calls me back to the Beginning, the place of my very essence, my very soul. That place that exists in all of us. That place which we walk blindly to called Home."

Chapter 31

REFLECTIONS

 Can you say, 'Let thy will be done' and mean it, and be willing to do whatever I ask you to do, no matter how strange or foolish it may appear in the eyes of others? It takes courage and such deep inner knowing and certainty that nothing will be able to throw you off balance. Only those souls who are strong will be able to follow this spiritual path.

Eileen Caddy

In working with Annie and in writing this book, I gave myself the greatest gift of all. For in digging for the truth behind the stories I have shared with you, I inadvertently discovered a piece of myself hidden away since birth. It has helped explain the anger and the feelings of danger lurking in the shadows of my being. These feelings have been rising more and more to the surface as the light has become more insistent each day.

Brenda refers to this act of discovery as housecleaning. For the longest time I did not realize that what I was saying to those who know me best is, "But I don't do windows."

Now I knew I must. Recently I invited my

father's memory back into my life and asked him to take me by the hand and return together to Stephen, Minnesota, and the first five years of my life, much of which I have had difficulty remembering.

We sat together at the kitchen table in the lodge at Potter's Farm, my father's memory and I, working up our courage. And while we sat there, even though I felt he was not there in spirit as my mother had been at Findhorn, I was able to imagine what he might have said to me after all of these years.

He would have apologized for not loaning me that 300 bucks I needed to finish my Ph.D. course work in the 70's. He would know now that spending $3000 on a crypt instead (really just a drawer in the wall of a mausoleum) was stupid. He would say he saw me sitting there on the floor of this building in front of this damn drawer crying my eyes out after Mom died and they were both, for crying-out-loud, head to toe in the same drawer. And I was Ph.D.-less and motherless and fatherless and sitting on a fake grass carpet inside a cold stone building instead of on a grassy hill. And all because of this mixup in priorities.

He would also say that he was so proud of me because I'd given up cigarettes all those years ago and not let alcohol get the best of me, things he couldn't do in his lifetime (but bloody well intended to do in the next go-round, I'll bet).

He'd also admit he understands how the game of life works now and how needless it was that he got so wrought up over the choice I made to divorce in the early years. And how my life has been one big mountain climbing expedition and he sees the bigger picture. And that he likes what he sees.

I'd say "I understand now why there were upsets over the divorce and my decisions regarding the children. I could have done better if I had been wiser, Dad. And I don't want to have to do this trip with you, because I like the memory of you just the way it's been. But I need to get to the beginning, to the first years so I can come clean and you can come clean."

What I finally had to say was, "Dad, it's time to go back there now. We've got to face what happened so I can get on with my life. I don't think you abused me in physical ways but I know I have to see what did happen to all of us in those years. It's time to feel safe in the present moments of my life."

As he took my hand I got smaller and smaller until I was my grandson's age and he was my son's age. He said, "I hurt her several times, you know, I drank a lot." I looked way up at him and saw that he was young and I loved him very much.

Then I was in that apartment building next to the river. I was in the bedroom in my crib and I was standing up, holding on for dear life because there were shouts and banging on the other side of the wall. And I was terrified for Mommy and terrified for Daddy.

Suddenly the door crashed open and he lurched through the door. He saw my face and through the fog he saw the tears of fear streaking my cheeks and he knew he'd hurt me just as deeply as he'd ever hurt anybody and he couldn't stand it. Because he never meant to hurt anybody in the first place.

Then I got a bigger picture of what it was like. That tiny apartment was suffocating. That little space was filled with anger and sorrow and pain. And as I got bigger and could walk and run, I tried to come to the rescue. I knew I had tried to rescue them throughout the later years, but I hadn't realized how I started rescuing so soon. What I really needed was for them to come to my rescue.

That apartment was nice in the daytime, but night was hell because you never knew what was coming. When the hours of fury and silence and crying and recrimination were over, I'd fall all over them to get love and to give love. As the fear for my mother got stuffed further inside and the anger over my father's anger got stuffed inside on top of it, I got stronger and stronger and I got tougher. I got really good at bluffing, at going around saying to the world, "I dare you. Go ahead and hit me. Hurt me. I dare you. I'm no weakling. I'm strong."

My father never laid a hand on me all the years of our lives, drunk or sober, except once when I said to my mother "I hate you!" I was 15 and he, sober as a judge, came into the kitchen and slapped my face and said, "Don't ever say those words again." So anger was never to be expressed. And fear was never to be shown — except in safe places.

And where were those?

So I did what many children do. I spent years trying to please and perfecting the pleasing song and then teen years rehearsing the rebellion dance. This song and dance trotted me right on into adulthood and came to be called the tango between mush and harshness.

Dad's memory and I sat on two stones in the woods and reflected upon what I had just uncovered. "Boy, buddy, does it take a heap of work to get clear enough to be able to shed all this luggage we cart around in the name of the past," I wailed. "If we carried around all the physical objects we have ever accumulated over a lifetime we would eventually be buried in an avalanche of crud. Why is it any different with our past, with our memories? They can bury us too. Without our even knowing it. No forgiveness, no forgetting. Just wagons full of years of fear slowing us down 'til we stop. Time to drop dead. Oh Dad, I knew you taught me unconditional love but I just now learned that it was also from you that I first experienced anger and fear."

I said goodbye to my father's memory that day, still loving him as always. I wished him Godspeed and blessings on whatever path he was now on. But before his memory moved on, I thanked him for helping me to see the lessons in safety. First, that safety comes in honoring ourselves and secondly, that safety lives in the arena of unconditional love which must be love without judgement. When we feel truly safe, we can then confront that fearful ego side of self, that dark and desperate controlling side that practices the dance of harshness. Or that part of us that turns to mush and we can't speak up.

Dad's lessons have led me through a year of self-discovery. I have been gifted with many people this past year who have mirrored for me the dance, so I can finally some day get it and let it go. Some of these experiences have been transforming for all involved. Some have gotten stuck without resolution. Others have transformed in an instant or required a great deal of work. In one case my partner/teacher, Dan, was so fully unconditional in his love and acceptance that I was able to make leaps in understanding that heretofore would have taken months or perhaps years.

True partnership as well as community is not free of the shadow side of self. But the environment is wholly safe and participants celebrate the strengthening of one another without the necessity of guilt or blame. What a wondrous world we will create when we are able to manifest such communities and partnerships throughout the planet.

Chapter 32

BLINDWALKING THE PATHWAY OF UNITY

 Our joyful task is to keep making more and more connections in good relationship with each other and All Things. As the old way begins to crumble and fall away from beneath our feet, we will find ourselves dancing high on the exquisite rainbow bridge of unity — the gossamer bridge that could not even be seen until the light of the new day, and the dust of the crumbling old ways, make it evident. In that new day, we will look toward the horizon, and see White Buffalo Calf Pipe Woman come singing. And it will be good.

Brooke Medicine Eagle

I continue to study and practice *A Course in Miracles*. It is an essential part of my journey, my particular path. I believe the Course is here to create more teachers for God at a very difficult time on the earth. And I believe all of us are potentially teachers and messengers for God. I understand that *A Course in Miracles* is not for everyone, and people seem to know whether it is or isn't for them. There are many paths to God.

I also continued from the first message forward to listen to the voice within and write down what I heard. The messages have been central in my life for over eight years now and became, among other things, the vehicle for understanding this journey to a place we now call Potter's Farm. The uplifting, supportive messages have been joined by detailed, informational messages as well. This practice is available to all, and Ann and others who have visited Potter's Farm have joined me in recording their own guidance on a daily basis.

The study and messages have been fleshed out with meditation, prayer, visualization, drawings, work with sound and music, as well as ritual and ceremony. Much ceremony is drawn from various Native or Aboriginal traditions. I have been fortunate to work with three men who have assisted me in traveling the Good Red Road through pipe ceremony and the sweat lodge. The pipe I was given is sacred to me and an honor to bear.

For me, the sweat lodge is a tiny church, and the people its living altar. The dark heat of the lodge is a powerful connection for heartfelt prayer with the Almighty. Spirit abides in the darkness and heat.

The rainbow teachings of Brooke Medicine Eagle, a friend from the old days whom I now meet through her music and words, has inspired me to be open to the Red Road as well. And Midge, from the Red Cliff band of Chippewa, takes women to her sacred fire for prayers with the grandmother Nokomis and all are welcome there. We share our journeys and prayers in the circle as equals. I bless these teachers.

These experiences have all added to my inner knowing and my intuitive self. I realize that my life and work have afforded me much more freedom and alone time for inner work than I have ever known before. My gratitude for this lifestyle is constant. But even when I am on the run I have learned the hard way that we must continually live in awareness of our inner selves or face becoming imbalanced and vulnerable.

I learned the importance of the Letting Go Ceremony while in a workshop in Open Space with Ginger Swain in 1989. All of the participants supported each person in song as, one at a time, we walked forward to the fire to release pain, guilt, illness, anger or whatever blockage needed to be released. I chose to affirm the release of cancer in my body and released as well the need for ego to be in the lead in my journey.

Following this experience, and on the advice of Tom Thiss, another open space friend, I created a black letting-go box. Mine was fashioned out of a shoe box and contains a statement I wrote that is read out loud to Creator each time I put an object or symbol of a problem into the box. It reads:

"May the Holy Spirit guide me in the ceremony of the Black Box. Into Your hands I release the contents of this box. Each object or symbol is from the past and I wish to let go of this past and be released in the spirit of true freedom. I fully understand and acknowledge that, in letting go, I allow the truth to overtake these illusions and I allow the universe to unfold in greater truth as well. My gratitude for your prayer and protection."

My black box has been filled to overflowing and many tears of release have been shed over its contents. But the rule is that once the box has claimed the new object, it is resolved into the light. I may look through the objects at any time, but they are no longer mine to worry over.

I continuously feel blessed by becoming more grounded to Earth and using centering and balancing through visualization and invocations. It is good when our beginning daily thoughts are of standing firmly upon Mother Earth, and connecting strongly with Universal Sky, focusing upon the center of Beingness and requesting that all chakras be in balance, opening and closing as needed. I often invoke the light of Christ within and ask that I be a clear and perfect channel for good with the Light as my guide. At the same time we do these invocations we can pray for others' well-being on a daily basis, keeping in mind that we do not know what is ultimately for their best or highest good.

Science is demonstrating that there is observable power in prayer. This says volumes to us about the power of our thoughts and how we direct our energy on a daily basis. Therefore, the peacefulness of long silent periods and visions that occur in meditation are a blessing as well.

And I've learned that healing takes a lot of effort on our own part, whether it be physical, emotional, mental or spiritual healing. We must consciously seek help from the Above (Spirit), the Below (Gaia), as well as the Within (our Higher Selves). When we are healed our mind becomes Mind, connected with the Universal Mind and with all our relations: two-legged, four-legged, winged, finned and creepy crawlies. And then there is no more room for fear and separation. Indeed! Fear and separation cease to exist. We are free of them. We are as the Butterfly who has transformed. We have moved into the New.

Ego fights for all it's worth to prevent our healing, for when we heal the ego is no longer in charge. What holds us back is the fear, the separation. In that state the miraculous cannot come. It too would be feared. In order to heal we must *choose* to heal. We must be willing to release our earthbound thoughts and stand empty awaiting the new. In this state of emptiness God comes. Of that there is no doubt. Willingness and Trust are our tools. Release is our process. Authentic love is our reward.

The notion of right-mindedness as explained by the Course and elaborated upon by Ken Wapnick, a scholar of the Course, has translated for me into notions of openness to the will of God as well. It seems that when we align ourselves with the will of God, synchronicity abounds. In actuality, the four rules of Open Space, slightly modified, seem to apply: we manifest right timing, right people, right events and right outcomes — all by being open to it.

My intuitive self is flourishing instead of languishing because I now feel the freedom to use all of my gifts. These traditions and innovations plus *A Course in Miracles* have freed me to see beyond the physical world to the world of Spirit, to know that our true Self is of Spirit, not body. And to know that when we but become open to it, Spirit lives beyond our earthly deaths and is every bit as real as we think this existence is.

The voice in the bookstore continues to remind me, "you have to do it alone." And indeed I believe we do. Most of us are not fortunate enough to have gurus in our backyard, or finely tuned prescriptions for spiritual success. But we have the ability to go within and rely upon the wisdom of our Higher Self. We have the opportunity to start over again and again, to risk more than the day before, to be more willing than we dared to be, and to consciously choose to be more loving. We have the freedom of choice in all things. And what we choose creates the quality of our future with God as with all else.

I am reminded of the wisdom of a three year old who sat at our kitchen table eating lunch with his parents and Bob one day this summer. Tim was chewing his sandwich thoughtfully and staring at Bob who he had just met, when he announced in a clear voice, "Bob, I'm planning on loving you." For Tim it is as simple as that. We have much to learn from him.

So what *is* blindwalking? Blindwalking is choosing one's perception to be on the side of Truth, as opposed to illusion. It is recognition that not being a body is a powerful notion of Truth that translates into our life in most practical ways. It is putting faith in the outcome ahead of every other consideration. It is going against every rule we were ever taught for survival. Blindwalking is renegade thinking to the very limits of imagination. It is walking into open space with a smile and a clown nose. It is hearing the voice in the cornfield and

trusting that voice more than any other. It is break-
ing the laws of economic gravity, and the grave-
ness of gravity and the pull toward the grave and
the graphic nonsense of our lives by creative high
play and new Holy Space for all to enter in. It is,
indeed, believing in our Selves for the first time,
and moving toward that purpose that sings its song
to us in the wind and the sea and on the wings of
thought — overruling that piece of us from the old
world that tells us it's a siren song. Blindwalking
is knowing that only in admitting our blindness
are we able to see truth. And only in our love, do
we conquer the fear of the world.

Chapter 33

OPENING TO LOVE

 The roads this world can offer seem to be quite large in number, but the time must come when everyone begins to see how like they are to one another.

A Course in Miracles

In this ending are new beginnings. I'm just truly beginning to understand that strength is not something of which we should be ashamed. That's our warrior side. I picture Eagle at my warrior side flying with me in illumination and courage.

But I also know we need balance and the gentleness of unconditional love. So I picture Dolphin on my feminine side. With that balance it's possible to be gentle and strong at the same time. Then it also becomes possible to love one another unconditionally and challenge one another to be the best that we can be by being honest in our love. We each need kindness and honesty from one another, not mush or harshness.

Jesus is an outstanding example, even if we can't believe all that has been written about Him. The standard he set for us two thousand or so years ago says to me that He got it. He really got it. He was a revolutionary who taught us who we really are. He asked us to see beyond the immediate into higher dimensions. He knew that our minds got boggled, but our intuition could inspire us to greatness and to remembrance of our ancient Truth. I don't think He wants us to worship Him. I think He wants us to get it, too. I think He wants us to be like He was. And you've got to know that isn't going to be easy. It's a damn hard journey, learning to be Christlike. And he got it in only 33 years. Geez!

And then there's Buddha and Lao Tzu and Black Elk and Ghandi and Sai Baba, just to name a few. All trying to show us what's possible. Truth is Truth no matter what form. It's Universal and just Is.

But, in our fear, what do we do? We run around in the name of Truth under some seventeen thousand different banners, separating ourselves and trying to outdo one another and turning the challenge to be who we are into pablum and pseudo-safety. Or sometimes violence.

We insist we each have a handle on Truth. And if Truth doesn't fit for us we make it fit. And we try to fit everybody into our definition of what is okay and what isn't. And to hell with what's been said about Love and Forgiveness and Higher

Selves and the ultimate challenge we have: to believe we are made in the image of our Creator.

Eric Fromm said that love is not primarily a relationship with a specific person. He said it's an attitude, an orientation to the world as a whole. He believed that love is an activity, a power of the soul.

And our Creator is Love.

Therefore, so are we.

The Course states, "A universal theology is impossible, but a universal experience is not only possible but necessary." So when are we going to get started? And when are we going to get it right for the children?

That leads straight back to each of us. The journey begins within. It begins the minute we come to this earth plane.

Brenda had a powerful dream one night, and the dream became a waking vision. She drew and wrote all night long, and in the morning she had an Earth Life Wheel so powerful in its message that she had to go back to bed just to rest from her labors. This is what she now shares on behalf of the children: "The four pieces of the heart of the Great Spirit are Wisdom, Trust, Peace and Self-Value. The ways we can encourage a new life to grow and deepen in each piece are as follows.

Wisdom
 Maintain an openness to the voice of the Spirit
 Stay tuned to Nature
 Listen to the Elders

Trust
 Recognize with respect your Personal Power
 Face the future with Confidence
 Realize that you can positively affect History

Peace
 Nurture your inner core of Faith
 Tune into the center of Calm
 Restore constantly with Universal Energy

Self-Value
 Accept the gift of your being with Respect
 Honor who you are with a life expressed
  with Integrity
 Be like no other, appreciate your Individuality
These are the Gifts of the Great Spirit to each
of us as we begin our journey here. We need each
other in order to remember and claim these gifts.
Each infant has one chance. Each individual act
of love, support and encouragement is essential
to fulfill that life to the promise that lies within."

 Mii-gwitch (thank you), Brenda.

EPILOGUE — PROLOGUE

And what of Potter's Farm?

Annie and others' healing experiences on the farm have strengthened my belief that Potter's Farm is indeed a place of healing. But we must recognize that although healing comes in many forms, it is ultimately the mind that must heal. Our species is just on the cusp of understanding this ancient Truth, I believe.

Findhorn speaks of the need for other centers of light throughout the world. Through our deep connection with Findhorn's messages of hope, I cherish the possibility that Potter's Farm is a progeny of Findhorn as well.

Beyond this, we truly do not know exactly what Potter's Farm is or how it will ultimately unfold. Through the process of blindwalking I have learned to trust that knowing all of the details is unnecessary. Where we have been relates to where we are now which relates to where we are going, but rather than seeing it as a linear process I see the wheel and the spiral dance. The music of the spheres plays an enchanting melody of hope which calls to increasing numbers. Potter's Farm is unfolding perfectly, and beyond that we need not be concerned.

Annie's guides have sent me a message of love to share with you:

Indeed we say...this manuscript will reach many who have and will choose at a teaching moment to hear the voice for God and once again align with Spirit and undertake to make their own lives a journey into a new direction...The choice made for God is one that insures richness of life, joy of one's spirit and the ultimate realization of one's true identity which is Divinity.

May your path be filled with Spirit, your heart overflowing with integrity, and your eyes and mind open to the Truth of who you are.

THE END
AND
THE BEGINNING

CHAPTER NOTES

a. Eileen Caddy, *Opening Doors Within*, copyright © 1986, Findhorn Press, Scotland.

b. <u>Prologue</u>: Copyright © 1987 by the estate of Brenda Ueland. Reprinted from *If You Want to Write* with the permission of Graywolf Press, Saint Paul, Minnesota.

c. <u>The Origin of Blindwalking</u>: Selected excerpt from *A Return To Love* by Marianne Williamson. Copyright © 1992 by Marianne Williamson. Reprinted with permission of HarperCollins Publishers Inc. Portions reprinted from *A Course in Miracles*. Copyright © by Foundation for Inner Peace, Inc. All chapter openings are from *A Course in Miracles*.

Reprinted with permission of the publisher. From *Reawakening The Spirit In Work*. Copyright © 1993 by Jack Hawley, Berett-Koehler Publishers Inc., San Francisco, California. All rights reserved.

Part One - The East and Awakening

Ch.1 <u>Two Beings On A Leaf</u>: *A Course in Miracles*, text, page 605. (Note: all page references from three volume hard cover set.)

Ch.2 <u>Independence Day</u>: Selected excerpt from *Power Through Constructive Thinking* by

Part Two - The South and Growth
Ch.4 <u>Agnes of God</u>: *A Course in Miracles*, Text, p. 132.
Ch.5 <u>On Our Way to Where?</u>: Richard Bach, *Illusions*, Dell Publishing Company, Inc., 1977.
Ch.8 <u>Endings, Emptiness and Beginings:</u> William Bridges, *Transitions*. Copyright © 1980 Addison-Wesley Publishing Company Inc.

Part Three - The North and Clarity
Ch.10 <u>Old Gives Way To New</u>: *A Course in Miracles*, text, p. 1.
Ch.11 <u>The Course and the Messages</u>: *A Course in Miracles*, text, p. 1. Kenneth Wapnick, Ph.D., *Absence From Felicity*, Foundation For A Course In Miracles, 1991.
A Course in Miracles, text, p. 71.
Ch.12 <u>Open Space</u>: *A Course in Miracles*, workbook, p. 305.
Harrison Owen, *Open Space Technology, A*

User's Guide. et al.

Ch.13 VanGo: *A Course in Miracles,* text, p.378-379.

Ch.15 Inklings: *A Course in Miracles,* text, p. 277.

Ch.16 The Vision: Eileen Caddy, Ibid.

Ch.17 New Horizons: *A Course in Miracles,* text, p. 524.

Ch.18 New Reality: Eileen Caddy, Ibid.

Ch.19 Commitment: E.E.Cummings, *Collected Poems* 1923-1954. Harcourt Brace and Company, 1960. Reprinted by permission of Liveright Publishing Corporation.

Ch.20 Birthing: Jamie Sams and David Carson, *Medicine Cards,* Bear and Company, 1988.

Ch.21 Scotland: M. Scott Peck, *A Different Drum,* Simon and Schuster, 1987.

Selected excerpt from *The Magic of Findhorn* by Paul Hawken. Copyright 1975 by Paul Hawken. Reprinted by permission of HarperCollins.

Selected excerpt from *The Findhorn Garden* by the Findhorn Foundation. Copyright © 1975 by the Findhorn Foundation. Reprinted by permission of HarperCollins Publishers Inc.

Ch.22 A Gift of Healing: Templeton quote reprinted with permission from Business Ethics Magazine, 52 S. 10th St., Suite 110, Minneapolis, Minnesota, 55403.

Ch.23 Spring and Renewal: From *Writing Down The Bones* by Natalie Goldberg, copyright © 1986. Reprinted by arrangement with Shambhala Publications, Inc. Massachusetts Avenue, Boston, Massachusetts 02115.
Emmet Fox, Ibid.

Part Four - The West and Birth
Ch.25 John: Richard Bach, Ibid.
Ch.26 Ritual of Love: *A Course in Miracles*, manual, p. 87.
Ch.27 The Move: Selected excerpt from *Mutant Message Down Under* by Marlow Morgan. Copyright © 1991, 1994 by Marlow Morgan. Reprinted by permission of HarperCollins Publishing Inc.
Ch.28 Brander Meets Associates: *A Course in Miracles*, manual, p. 85.
Ch.29 A Loving Lesson In Timing: Eileen Caddy, Ibid.
Ch.30 Partners In Grace: *A Course in Miracles*, workbook, p. 130.
Ch.31 Reflections: Eileen Caddy, Ibid.
Ch.32 Blindwalking the Pathway of Unity: Brooke Medicine Eagle, *Buffalo Woman Comes Singing*, Ballantine Books, a division of Random House Inc., 1991.
Ch.33 Opening To Love: *A Course in Miracles*,

text, p. 608. A Course in Miracles, manual, p. 73.

Brenda Dettmann, *Earth Life Wheel*, copyrighted © 1995.

BIBLIOGRAPHY

A Course in Miracles, Foundation for Inner Peace, 1975.

Bach, Richard, *Illusions*, Dell Publishing Co. Inc., 1977

Bridges, William, *Transitions: Making Sense of Life's Changes,* Addison Wesley, 1980.

Brooke Medicine Eagle, *Buffalo Woman Comes Singing*, Ballantine Books, 1991.

Business Ethics, "Interview: Sir John Templeton", Vol. 8, No. 6, Nov/Dec., 1994.

Caddy, Eileen, *Opening Doors Within*, The Findhorn Press, 1987.

Cummings, E.E., *Poems, 1923-1954*, Harcourt, Brace and Co., 1960.

Dettmann, Brenda, *Earth Life Wheel*, Copyright, 1995.

Findhorn Community, *The Findhorn Garden*, Harper and Row, 1975.

Fox, Emmet, *Power Through Constructive Thinking*, Harper and Brothers, 1940.

Goldberg, Natalie, *Writing Down the Bones*, Shambhala Press, 1986.

Hawken, Paul, *The Magic of Findhorn*, Harper and Row, 1975.

Hawley, Jack, *Reawakening the Spirit in Work*, Berrett-Koehler, 1993.

Morgan, Marlow, *Mutant Message Down Under*, Harper-Collins, 1991.

Owen, Harrison, *Open Space Technology, A User's Guide*, Abbott Publishing, 1992.

_____, *Leadership Is*, Abbott Publishing, 1990.

_____, *Riding the Tiger*, Abbott Publishing, 1991.

Peck, M. Scott, *A Different Drum*, Simon and Schuster, 1987.

Sams, Jamie and David Carson, *Medicine Cards*, Bear and Company, 1988.

Skutch, Robert, *Journey Without Distance*, Celestial Arts, 1984.

Ueland, Brenda, *If You Want To Write*, Graywolf Press, 1987.

A Note From the Author

The author welcomes inquiries concerning book orders, seminars and other presentations plus updates regarding Potter's Farm. Please address these inquiries to Brander and Associates, P.O. Box 864, Washburn Wisconsin, 54891.

Additional copies of *Blindwalk To Potter's Farm* may be obtained from the above address by enclosing $14.95 plus $2.50 shipping and handling. (Wisconsin residents: add 5.5% sales tax or an additional $.82.) Please make checks payable to Brander and Associates.